I Am the Lord Who Heals You

Reflections on Healing, Wholeness, and Restoration

EDITED BY
G. SCOTT MORRIS, MD

Abingdon Press
Nashville

Library of Congress Cataloging-in-Publication Data

I am the Lord who heals you : reflections on healing, wholeness, and restoration / G. Scott Morris, editor.
  p. cm.
  ISBN 0-687-06658-1 (pbk. : alk. paper)
  1. Spiritual healing—Sermons. 2. Sermons. 3. Spiritual healing—Biblical teaching.
I. Morris, G. Scott, 1954- II. Title.
  BT732.512 2004
  252—dc22

2004018988

To the staff of the Church Health Center.
Your works of healing have helped thousands of people who
were wounded and in need.

Acknowledgments

Prior to working on this book, I didn't understand why books had acknowledgment pages that most people just skip over. But after working on several manuscripts, it is crystal clear to me that many people's efforts are needed to create a successful book. I am first thankful to the authors who contributed sermons. Each member of this group is from the A-list of preachers I have heard in my life. While some of them are famous, they all have the charisma required to be leaders in the faith community. I am grateful to all of them for their willingness to be included in this collection.

Nancy Wiers, my personal assistant at the Church Health Center, has helped greatly to coordinate many of the logistics of bringing the manuscript together. My thanks go to Patti Russell for encouraging Abingdon to publish the collection and to Jill Reddig at Abingdon for championing the project and holding my hand along the way. Finally, I cannot thank enough my long-time associate, Barbara Lindstrom, who bird-dogged this project from day one. It was she who made sure that all the *i*'s were dotted and the *t*'s crossed and kept encouraging all of us to stay on track and meet our deadline. Even more, through it all, she has been my friend.

Contents

ix

Introduction

For many people in the faith community, the mention of healing evokes memories of Oral Roberts on TV in the 1950s and 1960s. For people younger than thirty, the idea of healing is only associated with the health-care industry. Yet neither image is an accurate reflection of the faith community's vital role in the well-being of our bodies and spirits.

Healing is a concept central to the Judeo-Christian witness of God's presence in the world. One third of the Bible is concerned with providing relief from disease and sickness. Yet for most people, the healing ministry of the church or synagogue is relegated to a bygone era. Many insist that the body is the subject of science and medicine while the spirit is the sole realm of the community of faith. This distinction is artificial and the consequence of the philosophical suppositions of Plato and Descartes.

Intuitively, however, most people realize that what affects one's spirit affects one's body and vice versa. In my role as a physician, I daily see patients who have a physical complaint that is generated by a spiritual problem. On the other hand, serious diseases can have devastating consequences to our spiritual well-being. The health of the body and the spirit are intimately connected.

This collection of sermons is a reflection of the belief that the faith community has an important role to play in the realm of healing. Healing is not solely the purview of people who wear white coats. In fact, I feel certain that effective healing requires the nurture of the spirit, and that the community of faith is far more suited to offer such care than the medical profession.

The sermons in this collection come from some of the world's best-known preachers as well as pastors in community congregations. The theological points of view are very diverse. I suspect I could not get the sixteen preachers to agree on the price of a cup of coffee, yet each of them passionately feels the need for people of faith to be involved in an active healing ministry.

The charge for each contribution was simple. Give me your best sermon on healing. How healing was defined was left up to the preacher. As you will see, how one interprets the meaning of healing is not universal, but there is strong agreement that it is the responsibility of the faith community to be always in the midst of people's brokenness, whether in body or spirit.

I find it interesting that almost all of the sermons were written after 9/11 but that only Michael Lapsley, the chaplain to Nelson Mandela and the African National Congress, wrote about healing the worldwide wounds caused by this day in history. Several sermons focus on the wounds caused by death. William Sloane Coffin's sermon after the death of his son, Alex, is a truly famous sermon on the presence of God in the midst of our deepest sorrow. It is a privilege to include it in this collection.

Each sermon speaks of healing from a slightly different theological perspective. There are conservative evangelicals and liberal Protestants in the mix; academic teachers of preaching and ministers who preach from the same pulpit week after week. The perspectives of women, minorities, and mainline congregations are all represented.

What I hope the reader will take away from this collection is the deeply held belief that the issue of healing permeates our relationship with God at almost every level. The body that God has given us is more than an empty shell that holds our spirit. The body is instead an integral part of the relationship we have with the Creator. When it is broken or diseased, the spirit suffers. When the spirit is bruised, the body is disturbed. Healing is a daily process that teaches us to be more fully in communion with God. Healing must not be relegated to physicians and the health-care system. Instead, the faith community is expected to make healing a central issue in all matters of hope, love, and compassion. The common thread through each sermon is this very notion. Healing is a process, which seeks to make us whole, and our relationship with God is, in part, dependent on healing continually taking place.

G. Scott Morris
The Church Health Center
Memphis, Tennessee

— 1. —
Healing and Its Opponents

Exodus 15:19-26; Mark 3:1-6

WALTER BRUEGGEMANN

The exodus story is an account of immense suffering, of caring drama, and of stunning deliverance. The Israelites were helpless before the brutal power of Pharaoh. But then God came! God intervened! God saw, heard, knew, and intervened (Exod. 2:23-25; 3:7-8). There followed a contest between the empire and the God of well-being (Exod. 5–11). Israel came through the waters to freedom and well-being (Exod. 14:30-31; 15:19). It is no wonder that Miriam and the other women took tambourines and danced their joy, their surprise, and their new health (Exod. 15:20-21).

The story of the exodus is focused on the power of Egypt, embodied by Pharaoh, the ruthless king, and expressed as arrogant power and brutal labor policy. This story in the Bible is given us by the slaves from the perspective of their helplessness. They know about and tell about real, raw, cynical, exploitative power. Pharaoh is portrayed by the slaves at his most cruel, but he does not seem to mind and cooperates fully with this brutal image offered of him.

In the Bible, however, Pharaoh is always more than a historical agent. Pharaoh becomes a metaphor and representative of all that could be wrong and distorted in the life of the community. More than historical agent, Pharaoh is the point person for a complete religious-economic system, a system that makes some safe, happy, and powerful at the expense of others who stay poor, helpless, and hopeless. More than in an imperial system, Pharaoh is presented as a demonic power that sets out deliberately to disable his victims who are not only his workforce but also a threat and, therefore, an enemy to be resisted and abused.

But more than system or even demonic system, in the religious imagination of ancient Israel, Pharaoh is anti-God who opposes all that God wants for Israel.

God wants life, Pharaoh wills death;
God wants joy, Pharaoh wants grief;
God wants wholeness, Pharaoh wants disability;
God wants hope, Pharaoh wants despairing compliance.
Pharaoh is anti-God, anti-life, anti-health!

We may reflect on the "anti" quality of Pharaoh by considering only two of God's Ten Commandments that Pharaoh actively, systemically opposes.

God said, "Remember the sabbath day" (Exod. 20:8-11), but Pharaoh decreed that Israelite slaves should always work and never rest.

God said, "You shall not covet" (Exod. 20:17), but Pharaoh engaged in endless acquisitiveness in effective, systemic ways. No wonder Pharaoh is viewed by Israel as anti-life and anti-health!

And then comes the God of Israel who in great love and in equally great power engaged in a contest with Pharaoh that we call "plagues" (Exod. 5–11). In a most dramatic way, Pharaoh and his system of death are overthrown. Israel walks safely through the waters until it can dance and sing. The slaves are "free at last." And then, just as the exodus story is about to end, God makes one more announcement in one of the longest verses in the Bible (Exod. 15:26).

God gives a self-announcement and asserts, "I am the LORD who heals you." Or it could as well be translated, "I am the lord, your doctor." The entire exodus story of conflict and emancipation is understood here as a healing by God, a restoration to full function of the community of Israel after being severely disabled by Egyptian abuse.

2

Now the importance of this interpretive angle is that the crisis of disability caused by Pharaoh and the gift of healing offered by God are lined out in large and systemic terms. It is often—too often—the case that healing is understood only in a personal or even a mechanical sense as the repair of a personal bodily element. While each of us, of course, is concerned with the full functioning of our bodies, it is crucial to recognize that real healing is a much larger deal. The God of the Bible is preoccupied with large social systems that produce disability, before which individual persons are completely helpless.

Thus in verse 26, "God the doctor" does not vaguely promise to heal but quite specifically has in view systemic illnesses referred to as the "diseases of Egypt." That phrase is not specific, and scholars have used great energy trying to identify the "diseases" for which we may receive clues from the plague narrative. If, however, we accept YHWH as a "systems doctor," then we may understand the "diseases of Egypt" as "systemic maladies" that come with the territory of large socioeconomic systems that have no capacity for human compassion.

Let us consider the "diseases of Egypt," imperial maladies, from the perspective of both "masters" (taskmasters and supervisors [Exod. 5:10]) and of "slaves." The "masters" who worked for Pharaoh were under immense pressure to produce, to meet quotas of brick production. We may imagine that such agents of the empire (the managerial class) are beset by greed to get ahead; by anxiety about failure that would lead to punishment, demotion, or both; and by general stress that is endemic to an exploitative economy. Those who participate in and benefit from such a system are almost inevitably caught in an endless round of restlessness, absence of sleep, and lack of real joy.

The "slaves," on the other hand, are said to have a "bad odor" (Exod. 5:21), a phrase that may refer to a feeling of social contempt. But the reference to odor may also signify a physical kind of bodily affront that comes with poverty, overwork, and the lack of a reasonable social structure, circumstances that issue in physical vulnerability and spiritual despair. The slave narrative portrays a population that is genuinely helpless. The unbearable

3

irony of course is that stressed managers and the hopeless slaves endlessly reinforce each other and deepen the disability of the other party in an endless vicious cycle; *stress* produces more work demands upon the slaves and *despair* makes slaves even less productive, resulting in greater stress, and on and on.

Then dramatically, into this vicious cycle comes "the doctor." The good news of the gospel is that the God of Israel takes such distorted social systems as the precise venue in which power relations can be transposed and chances for human wholeness can be enhanced. No wonder they sang and danced! They saw firsthand that wherever "holy healing" intervenes, the diseases of Egypt lose their defining power. YWWH makes it possible for the "managers" to desist from quota-driven anxiety and makes it equally possible for the "slaves" to escape from the pit of despair that makes human life impossible.

The exodus narrative is an attestation that the God of Israel, in ways visible and in ways not seen, has all the power of all creation to turn life to flourishing and well-being. This God works not only by one-on-one remedies but also by facing the systems of death and by robbing them of authority. It is the same God who is present in Jesus of Nazareth. And when Jesus heals the man with the withered hand in our story, the powers of status quo resist the healing:

> The Pharisees went out and immediately conspired with the Herodians against him, how to destroy him. (Mark 3:6)

The Pharisees are the moralists and the Herodians are the power people. The two together constitute opposition to God's healing as powerful and as poisonous as the old-time Pharaoh. Those who profit from old systems of imperial diseases are, of course, opponents of God's healing. But, say both the exodus narrative and Mark's account, the opponents of healing cannot stop the healing because, even in quite concrete cases of healing, all the powers of God's rule are effectively mobilized. The news about the killing power of brutality is the good news of healing that will not be stopped by its enemies.

Before the doctor quits speaking in 15:26, the doctor lays down some conditions for healing after Egypt. Like any doctor, this doctor is not a magic worker. Finally, health depends upon the capacities and disciplines of the "client," who in this case is Israel. Like a doctor who urges "dieting and exercise" as conditions of healing, so the God of the exodus pronounces an "if" over Israel's future health outside the Egyptian system:

> "If you will listen carefully to the voice of the LORD your God, and do what is right in his sight, and give heed to his commandments and keep all his statutes..."

The condition, not unlike dieting and exercise, is to do what the doctor prescribes. And what this doctor prescribes, the God of Sinai as of exodus, is the commandments of the Torah. The reference is to the Ten Commandments soon to be enunciated (Exod. 20:1-17), and all the derivative laws. These are the conditions of health, for health is not a careless offer given by the doctor but is a new possibility at which the "client" must work with intentionality:

"No other gods" (Exod. 20:3). This means not to be sucked back into loyalty to abusive systems like that of Egypt, even if they promise good, for it is a promise that cannot be kept.

"Honor your father and your mother" (Exod. 20:12). This is an insistence that family networks can be carriers of health where folks respect and nurture one another, for health cannot come to isolated individuals or to those who live an existence of alienation.

"You shall not murder. You shall not commit adultery" (Exod. 20:13-14). Distorted social relations, especially if defined by violence, preclude any alternative system of health.

"You shall not covet" (Exod. 20:17). That is, do not join the rat race, for even the winners in the rat race of success and acquisitiveness turn out to be rats.

It is evident that this "medical 'if'" permits us to receive God's commands very differently. Those commands are not random rules imposed by an arbitrary ruler. They are, rather, clues about the inescapable conditions of well-being in God's ordered universe. Nor is obedience blind conformity, but it is a disciplined enactment of prerequisites that will make for health and that will keep us from being seduced back into the systems of death that replicate Pharaoh.

Thus verse 26 is a rich and instructive statement that invites us to reshape our categories for health and to think large about healing:

"Egypt" means any abusive environment that is organized for profit and power against elemental human well-being;

"Egyptian diseases" are the predictable maladies that come by living life in abusive systems organized for profit and power;

The God of Israel, the one given us in Jesus Christ, is a transformative agent who breaks vicious power systems and creates alternative possibilities for well-being;

The commands of God are not inconveniences or arbitrary insistences but are the disciplines that receive God's intention for health and fend off the high costs of the systems of death.

This little verse invites us to think large and clearly about healing, to see God as the only power who can move effectively against death systems. There remains a great deal of human work to do in the face of such systems, human agents who replicate the Divine Doctor. But more important are the "clients," God's creatures who are summoned to the new health system that is elsewhere termed "the kingdom of God." That same health system protects "managers" from stress and "slaves" from despair. That system invites all members of the community to sing and dance together, "free at last," on the way to new lands of milk and honey.

WALTER BRUEGGEMANN is professor emeritus at Columbia Theological Seminary in Decatur, Georgia. His most recent books include *Inscribing the Text: Sermons and Prayers of Walter Brueggemann* and *Introduction to the Old Testament: The Canon and Christian Imagination*.

── 2. ──
From Victim to Victorious

MICHAEL LAPSLEY, SSM

Editor's Note: In 1990 in Zimbabwe, Father Lapsley opened a letter bomb. He lost both of his hands and one eye in the subsequent explosion.

I want to speak to you as a wounded person speaking to other wounded people. This is my first visit to the United States since the events on September 11, 2001. I want to say to you, particularly as people of New York, that I am sorry about what happened. I am sorry and it was wrong.

I wonder how each of us felt—not *thought*, but *felt*—on September 11 and in the days and the months that followed.

"I feel angry."
"I feel overcome with grief."
"I feel confused, I feel bitter."
"I want them to feel some of the pain that we feel."

What range of feelings have you experienced in your own hearts? Perhaps many of us have had many different feelings, sometimes contradictory feelings. Sometimes if we are part of the faith community, we are inclined to talk about the nice feelings that we have and not necessarily admit to ourselves and to others that we, too, have horrible feelings. How did we feel, when the bombing of Afghanistan began, when we began to see the images of other people in pain?

I would like to share with you a little today of what my own journey has been and some of what the journey has taught me. In April 1990, I became a victim of state terrorism through the decision of the state [of South Africa] to seek to kill me by placing a bomb inside the pages of two religious magazines. For reasons that doctors do not understand, I did not go into shock, I did not lose consciousness, when I opened the magazine and the bomb went off. And so I remember the pain. But I also remember the presence of God with me; that somehow, to me, the great promise of Scripture had been kept. Not a promise that we will not suffer because, of course, God does not promise us that, but instead the promise "Lo, I am with you always, even unto the end of the world" (Matt. 28:20 KJV). This is God's promise accompaniment, to be with us on our journey. I somehow felt that Mary, who watched her son being crucified, understood what it was that I was experiencing.

Because I had lived in the countries of southern Africa, but traveled the world during the last years of apartheid, when I was bombed I received messages of prayer, love, and support from all around the world.

I sometimes say that when I die I will not have a funeral because people said all the nice things at that time. I am not sure how much we hear at funerals, so I think it is better to have it said now. But that prayer, that love, that support was the vehicle that God used to enable me to make my bombing redemptive—to bring the life out of the death, to bring the good out of the evil, and to be able to walk a journey from victimhood to being a survivor, to becoming a victor.

You see, when something terrible is done to us, of course we are victims. If we physically survive, we are survivors. But often that is where people stop. The next step is not taken—to become a victor, to move from being an object of history to becoming once more a subject; to become what that wonderful word in Scripture speaks of as being cocreators, being the coworkers with Christ in building God's kingdom. You see, if something terrible happens to us, we never remain unchanged and unmarked. It will either diminish us or cause us to grow.

The great South African leader Chief Luthuli once said, "Those who think of themselves as victims eventually become the victimizers of others." And so the journey is either toward victims becoming victimizers—the continuation of the cycle—or the journey is toward becoming victorious, to live not according to the values of those who did these things to us but according to other values.

For those of us in the international community who watched with horror when the events of September 11 unfolded, we could not help having hearts filled with pain, compassion, and love. This was manifested so clearly in the Chapel of St. Paul at Ground Zero with all those thousands and thousands of messages of prayer, love, and support.

But the question of course was, "What would be the response?" On September 11, I was in Northern Ireland, and within an hour or two, amazingly, I managed to get through on the phone to New York City. Like most people everywhere, before my eyes came all the people I knew and loved who lived in the city. And so I spoke to two people within an hour. One person said to me, "I am frightened of what the response is going to be." The other person said to me, "It is too terrible, but it is a consequence of our policies."

I suppose also for me, while imprinted on me were the images of what we saw on September 11, there are other images. The nature of my ministry is that I get invited to places of pain. I am still waiting for someone to invite me to a place with no pain.

And so I have been to Rwanda. I have been in a church like this, filled with skulls, where six weeks earlier hundreds of thousands of people were killed. I have been to East Timor where a third of the population was killed during twenty-five years of Indonesian occupation. And you see, one of the things I have learned as I traveled the world is that history and politics and economics and sociology of countries are unique, but pain is pain, is pain, is pain, is pain. . . . And what we are capable of as a human family, in its beauty, joy, faith, hope, courage, and compassion and in its ugliness, hatred, bitterness, and the desire for revenge, is true everywhere.

9

It seems to me that as a country, the United States took the route of the victims becoming the victimizer. But I have met many extraordinary human beings, heroic human beings, who did not take, are not taking, have not taken that route. I could not help being filled with pride to hear that the bishop of this cathedral had initiated a project to build a mosque in Kabul.

I also met Imani Imani, a young African American woman, who lost her friend on September 11. She said that she was invited to go to some classes for grief, some sessions dealing with grief and mourning. She said to me, "You know, I could only go for about three days because I discovered that the classes were not about grief but about hatred and revenge." And then she said, "That is not what my friend was about."

I had the privilege of celebrating the Eucharist and preaching at the Chapel of St. Paul at Ground Zero. After I preached, a Nigerian man with his arm in a sling, who is a rescue worker there, came and spoke to me about what I had said and what my sermon meant to him.

Then a man came and knelt beside me as I sat in the pew. He gave me a cross made out of marble that had come from the twin towers.

I think often that the route to healing and wholeness is, in some ways, more difficult for the relatives of the victims than it is for the survivors. Because I think that sometimes the relatives of the victims feel that they owe it to their loved ones to keep hatred alive.

I remember in South Africa meeting a woman whose son had been killed fifteen years previously. When I met her I was struck by the ugliness of her face, physically contorted by hatred. She told the story of her child as if it happened but a second ago. I asked her what her child would have wanted for her as his mother. In the process of the workshop, she began to let him rest. Not to forget him, not to stop loving him, but to let him go and to let him rest. On the last day of the workshop, I could have walked past her because the lines of her face had changed. She became radiant. She had moved from being the relative of a victim to being a victor.

Our "westernness" often makes us think that this journey should be very fast, but our humanness should tell us that the journey to healing and wholeness is a long journey. I am sure there are many in this cathedral today who are still hurting very deeply inside. Perhaps for many of us there is still poison within us, poison that we are justified to have. If something terrible has happened to you, to those you love, it is an understandable and normal response to hate, to be bitter, to want revenge. The problem is, if we keep it inside us, it will destroy us. It will not destroy our enemies; it will destroy us. We have to find ways of acknowledging the poison and letting it go. That is a journey we need to travel.

You know, I sometimes feel that the greatest way the United States could avenge the Al Qaeda network and the people who become desperate enough to make bombs to kill so many human beings would be to create a different kind of America. That would be our real revenge.

I have a dream, as Martin Luther King Jr. had, that one day the United States will sing a new song. When it sings that song, there will be no more executions in this country. Again I am proud that my church, the Episcopal Church, is one so deeply opposed to the death penalty. But in my dream as well, the United States would lead the world in saying "an end to the debt." I have a dream that you, the richest and most powerful country in the world, will become a country in which there is no homelessness. I have a dream that your prisons will no longer be filled with African Americans and Hispanics/Latinos. I have a dream that you will pay not only your church collection but also your debt to the United Nations. In other words, my dream for you is that this great country would become a leader by its moral example, not by its military power. Because, in the end, you can have all the guns in the world, you can have "Star Wars," but while a huge part of humanity is hungry and desperate, you will have no security.

It is the New Testament that tells us as Christians what our way forward is. The New Testament speaks of the gentleness, the tenderness, and the kindness that we are called to have as our hallmarks. It speaks of the importance of conscience.

It may be that my dream will not be realized today or tomorrow, but I do believe that it will be realized someday. I hope that you, my brothers and sisters, will be like Imani, like the man who knelt beside me, like the Nigerian I saw, like the "9/11 Families for Peaceful Tomorrows."

I hope you will be the signs of hope in this land by how you live your lives. Our faith tradition says that at the end of time, there will be a day of judgment. I do not think God will ask any of us, "Did you sort out the problem of the United States? Did you sort out the problem of South Africa? Is the world a perfect place?" But God might say to us, "Did you recognize your own wounded-ness? Did you recognize your own fallen-shortness? Did you come to me and ask me to walk with you on your journey to healing? Is this world a gentler, kinder, more just place because you have walked this earth?"

Sometimes I ask myself, "Why did I survive when so many others with whom I participated in the struggle against apartheid died?" I cannot help answering that some of us had to survive to be signs of the truths of what we had done to one another. But much more important, in a small way, we are to be signs that in the end, the forces of God, of gentleness, of kindness, of justice, of compassion are stronger than the forces of the evil of war, of hatred, and of death.

MICHAEL LAPSLEY was born in New Zealand and trained as an Anglican priest in Australia before moving to South Africa where he worked as chaplain to Nelson Mandela and the African National Congress for fifteen years. He was exiled to Zimbabwe where, in 1990, he opened a letter bomb and lost both of his hands and one eye in the subsequent explosion. He now lives and works in Cape Town, South Africa, and is the director of the Institute for Healing of Memories. This sermon was preached at the Cathedral of St. John the Divine in New York City, May 5, 2002.

——3.——
Some Healing Is Up to You

John 5:1-9

MAXIE D. DUNNAM

There is a famous legend in Buddhist folklore in which the Buddha compares philosophical preoccupation with the matter of God's existence to a man shot with a poisoned arrow. Before the man would allow the arrow to be withdrawn, he insisted upon knowing who shot him, what kind of poison was in the arrow, who was going to administer the cure, and what was going to be the medication. Needless to say, he died before his questions were answered. The Buddha concluded that in the same way, people need to be rescued from suffering, craving, and ignorance, no matter how the issue of God's existence may fare among the philosophers.

Now the Buddha was right, but the legend has another truth. Debate and argument, precise doctrine, and rational understanding are not the answers to our salvation, and certainly not a prerequisite to healing, which is what we're considering in this sermon: healing. I want to talk specifically about the fact that some healing is up to you.

As the wounded man in the legend had to trust himself to the doctor in order to be cured, so you and I must trust ourselves, surrender ourselves to Jesus, in order that his grace might be sufficient for our healing.

Now the story of our Scripture lesson printed above is dramatic enough, and the lessons that are there, I believe, are rather clear. So let's move immediately to announce what those lessons are, and then explore them for our understanding.

1. *Jesus' ministry is a healing one;*
2. *The stance of faith is to accept any miracle Jesus wants to give; and*
3. *Some healing is up to us.*

First, let's simply record the fact that Jesus' ministry is a healing one. Throughout the Gospels, you will find those healing stories, which are like dramatic exclamation points in the totality of Jesus' ministry. I hope you quiver just a bit with excitement as we recall a couple of those healing stories.

Do your recall the story of the woman with a hemorrhage? Jesus was on his way to raise a little girl from the dead when this woman met him on the road. She was not dead like the girl that Jesus was going to raise, but she often wished she were dead. Her sickness was the kind of thing that was not only painful, it was embarrassing. It made her a social outcast. She had sought doctors in all the areas and had spent all her resources and all her energy trying to find the healing power that would relieve her of this malady, but to no avail. Now she had heard that Jesus was coming to town. She joined the multitude in going out into the village to see him, thinking that if she could just get close enough to him to touch him, maybe, just maybe, something would happen in her life like that which had been happening in the lives of others of whom she had heard. So she pressed through the multitude and drew close enough to reach out and touch just the hem of Jesus' garment. And it happened! She felt the power of Christ surging through her body, and the fountain of blood, which had flowed for years, ceased, and she knew herself to be healed. Jesus' ministry is a healing one (Mark 5:24-34).

Do you remember the man of the Gerasenes? He was possessed of demons to the point that he was compelled to dwell among the tombs. He called himself "Legion" because he said, "we are many" (Mark 5:9-10 RSV; see also Matt. 8:28-34). He knew there were powers within him that originated not from himself. He would often bruise himself with stones. He was lost in demonic darkness, had awful nightmares from which he thought he could

14

never escape. These forces within him were so powerful that the chains with which his friends bound him in order that he might not hurt himself, or hurt someone else, could not constrain him. He would break free of those chains.

And then it happened. Jesus came and spoke the healing word. The result is expressed in a sentence in the New Testament that is dramatic in its understatement: "And they came to Jesus, and saw the demoniac sitting there, clothed and in his right mind, the man who had had the legion" (Mark 5:15 RSV). Jesus' ministry is a healing one.

The parade could go on. The deaf, the blind, the mute, the lame—but now in the parade they hear, they see, their loosened tongues shout praise to God. They leap with joy because they've been healed.

You can't read any one of the Gospels without coming to this conclusion that Jesus' ministry is a healing one.

Now a second truth—the stance of faith is to accept any miracle Jesus wants to give.

"Now what's the connection?" you ask. And that's the right question. Because if we don't make this connection, it may very well be that we'll end up in bitterness or cynicism, maybe end up without faith, because we may find ourselves praying for the healing of persons, but those persons die. So what's the connection?

The connection is in the fact that not only are the miracles that Jesus gives us not always instantaneous but also that there are other miracles as well, and the stance of faith is to accept any miracle Jesus wants to give.

One of my predecessors as president of Asbury Theological Seminary, Dr. J. C. McPheeters, lived to be ninety-four. Dr. McPheeters was one of those rare, delightful persons that few of us are blessed to know. And I use one other descriptive word for him advisedly: eccentric. He learned to water-ski when he was seventy-five years old. On his eightieth birthday, he skied for twenty miles. He was one of those beautiful persons who come into the world like a breath of fresh air. He was a great evangelist, an effective preacher, a marvelous teacher, and the second president of Asbury Seminary. He was a person of prayer who exercised a ministry of healing for over fifty years. I feel honored to be his successor at Asbury.

One of the most outstanding lessons Dr. McPheeters taught us during his many years of public ministry was about healing. He said that from the Scriptures and from his own personal experience, he had learned that there are at least five miracles of healing that the Lord wants to give us.

First, there is the miracle of the instant cure. Many of us have seen it happen: the power of faith and the instrumentality of prayer have brought about instant healing. These have been proven medically and scientifically, but they are rare. Instantaneous healing, as a result of faith in prayer, is not the norm, though some would have you to believe that it is. One of the early participants in the Episcopal Healing Order of St. Luke's, Dr. Price, said that in his fifty years in a ministry of healing, he had witnessed thirty-seven instant healings. Even so, that's a miracle. Many studies have proved the influence of prayer in the healing process. That introduces the second miracle—what Dr. McPheeters called the miracle of God's undertaking. God undertakes by nature to heal us. An example of it is when a person cuts his thumb and doesn't do anything to it except to keep it clean and by a miracle of nature—God's nature—the body heals itself. God undertakes. He undertakes through doctors and nurses and medicine. He undertakes through other people to bring about healing in our lives. It's written into the very nature of things, and that's one of God's miracles.

Second, there is the miracle of God's leading us to the right cure for our malady. God sometimes leads us to a cure. He may lead us to a doctor, or a healing remedy, or a healing community. When it happens most of us readily confess God guided in this.

When Dr. McPheeters talked about this, he used an example from the life of King Hezekiah. The king was the victim of a boil that was sending poison throughout his body. The prophet Isaiah met with him and told him that he needed to prepare to die because death was imminent. The king, being a man of God, began to pray: "Remember now, O LORD, I beseech thee, how I have walked before thee in faithfulness and with a whole heart, and have done what is good in thy sight" (2 Kings 20:3 RSV).

Notice that he doesn't ask for God to heal him. He simply reminds God and states his position in relation to God. Use your imagination now as you see the prophet Isaiah leaving the king on his deathbed, praying and crying. Isaiah walks rapidly down the corridor, takes a swift right and then a left, down the steep steps into the inner courtyard of the castle. But then as he begins to enter the outside courtyard, he stops dead in his tracks. Something has happened; some word has come to him. He retraces his steps, finds a servant, and tells the servant to bring him a particular kind of fig. The servant brings the figs, and the prophet Isaiah mashes the figs together, makes a poultice, and puts it on the king's boil. And the king is healed. Three days later, the king is in the temple praying and praising God.

The truth of it is that God does perform miracles in our lives to lead us to a source of healing. Sometimes that miracle is God's leading us to a particular doctor or to a particular medication. Sometimes it is leading us to friends to whom we can pour out our hearts in order that the poison of our guilt might be relieved and our conscience might be salved. Sometimes it is leading us to a particular worship service where we hear the word of God preached, and by a miracle of the Spirit, that becomes God's blazing, transforming Word for us that day. Sometimes it is at the table of Holy Communion, when we take the bread and the wine, and we remember the presence of our Lord Jesus Christ, and we know that God has performed a miracle, a bringing together of the presence of his Son, Jesus, and us, in order that our lives might be made whole again. That is our third miracle.

Then, there is a fourth miracle: the miracle of the sufficiency of God's grace. Now mark this down: not all of us are going to be healed. Sometimes some of us are going to be given a circumstance that will stay with us forever—a painful circumstance, a suffering malady. Paul called it his "thorn in the flesh." I have an idea we don't think enough of the seriousness of what Paul was talking about; a thorn is such a little thing. The truth of the matter is that the same Greek word that we translate "thorn" can also be translated "stake." It was something big in Paul's life. It wasn't something little. It was something that he wrestled with day in and day out. It was a pain that plagued his conscience—spiritually and physically—day in and day out, to the point that he wrestled with God. He prayed ardently and passionately that somehow he would be delivered from that "thorn . . . in the flesh" (2 Cor. 12:7 RSV). But it didn't happen. He was not delivered. Yet, he said, "My grace is sufficient for you" (2 Cor. 12:9 RSV). That's a miracle—the sufficiency of God's grace.

I hope you get the chance to meet a man named Robert Standhardt. Robert was a longtime staff member of The Upper Room in Nashville. To hear Robert speak is a moving experience. He has a deep and powerful voice that has a resonance about it that moves you. He is a genius in his command of the English language. Someone said that compared to Robert Standhardt, Walter Cronkite appears to have laryngitis.

But there's something else about Robert Standhardt. He is about four and a half feet tall, and his body is the most disfigured, the most twisted, the most grotesque body I've ever seen. He's a quadriplegic—born that way. He has to thrust himself by all the strength he can muster in any kind of movement to get into his wheelchair. I first began to see him on sidewalks around The Upper Room in Nashville; I learned that he was an intern at the local veterans hospital. Having made the decision to preach, he received an academic scholarship to attend Perkins School of Theology at Southern Methodist University. He was completing his degree program by doing an internship in pastoral care at the veterans hospital.

I thought to myself, "People need to hear Robert Standhardt. The world needs to hear the message of this man, and especially persons across the nation with handicapping conditions need to be inspired by the grip that he has on life." I was then the world editor of The Upper Room, so I invited him to join our staff. For years he traveled all over the nation. You can't imagine the physical energy that he has to put forth just to take care of his physical needs—just to do those single things that you and I take for granted day in and day out. But whenever he received an invitation, whether it was in Iowa or California or New York, he would do everything required to get to his destination. When he spoke—usually hanging over his wheelchair because he has no control of his muscles, or sometimes remaining seated in his wheelchair—the glory of God was on his face and the power of the Christian message radiated through his words, and people knew the miracle of the sufficiency of God's grace.

Then there's the fifth miracle: the miracle of the triumphant crossing. You're not going to get out of this world alive, and death can be the passage from life to eternal life, if we know the miracle of a triumphant crossing. The ultimate healing miracle of God comes in the resurrection, because in the resurrection we'll enter a new kingdom. That's a miracle—a miracle God wants to give each of us.

The stance of faith is to receive any miracle God wants to give—whether the miracle of an instant cure, the miracle of God's undertaking, the miracle of God's guidance to a particular cure for our malady, the miracle of the sufficiency of God's grace, or that ultimate miracle of a triumphant crossing.

Now the final truth. There is some healing that is up to you. Go back to our third scripture lesson. This man had been at that pool with other invalids—blind, lame, paralyzed people. He had been afflicted for thirty-eight years, and had been waiting there a long time for the angel to trouble the water (John 5:3-5). Rehearse the story. Occasionally an angel would come stir the water. When the water was stirred, if you got into the water first, there would be a healing for you. This man had waited there for thirty-eight years.

Jesus shocked him with the question, "Do you want to be healed?" (John 5:6 RSV). Have you ever stopped to think, as you read this scripture, that the man never really answered Jesus' question? He could have said yes or no, but instead he took that opportunity to pour out his sad story of loneliness and disappointment and despair (John 5:7).

There is a lot in that story, but let's concentrate on this one point. Jesus asked him, "Do you want to be healed?" I believe that that is congruent with all that Jesus was, everything Jesus did, and everything Jesus said. He doesn't violate our freedom. He doesn't trample on our personhood. He invites us to be saved, to be healed. He calls us into his kingdom, but we have to make a response.

Now please understand what I am saying. I am aware of the fact that there are stories in the New Testament of people who are healed without any knowledge of the fact that Jesus is doing it. And there are stories about the faith of one person working for the healing sake of another. But in this instance, Jesus is saying, "Some healing is up to you." You have to participate; you have to desire it; it has to be an act of your will. Look at that man again. Had he lost hope? Had he settled down into a kind of negative despair? Or consider this possibility: Was he content in his illness because to be healed would mean he would have to take responsibility? He would have to begin to make decisions? He might have to begin to earn his living?

Does it shock you that I would suggest something like this? Are you a bit outraged that I would even think that this poor wretched man might not want to be healed? Let's be honest. I've known people who became content in their illness, people who used their illness to get their own way, to manipulate other people for their own self-satisfaction. I've known people who refused forgiveness and harbored resentment. I've known people who kept a hurt alive as a kind of tranquilizer. It's an odd sort of thing—their wanting to be in a victimized position in order that they could use the tools of their suffering to do battle with the world—and to do battle with others—to get their own way.

I remember counseling a woman who had that very problem with her mother, who was in a nursing home. Her mother did not want to be healed. As long as her mother was in that position, everybody in the family would coddle her, be extra attentive, respond to her at every beck and call. That's the situation Jesus was addressing when he asked, "Do you want to be healed?" Some healing is up to you, and Jesus is saying that sometimes it takes the will of a person, combined with Jesus' power, in order for the healing powers to be released in your life and mine.

Look at that man again. For years, he was at that pool waiting for the angel to come and the water to be stirred in order that he might be healed. For years he had waited and he had waited in vain. Why? Because Jesus was not there. If it's only a pool and an angel, you have to wait. Some are healed and some aren't. But when Jesus came, the man was healed. For thirty-eight years he had suffered. Why? Because it was only a pool and an angel. Jesus was not there.

Also, for years he had waited because he had not learned the lesson that some healing is up to us. And when you put those two things together—the presence of Jesus and the will to be healed—then you're ready; you're ready for any miracle Jesus wants to give.

And he'll give that miracle. He'll give that miracle for your healing and mine, or make his grace sufficient for us.

MAXIE D. DUNNAM is chancellor of Asbury Theological Seminary in Wilmore, Kentucky. He served as president of Asbury for ten years and was for many years a United Methodist pastor in Mississippi and Tennessee. Dr. Dunnam is the author of more than thirty books, including *This Is Christianity* and *The Workbook on the Ten Commandments*.

—— 4. ——
So You Want to Be Healed

Mark 1:40-45; 2 Kings 5:1-14

G. SCOTT MORRIS

A leper came to [Jesus] begging him, and kneeling he said to him, 'If you choose, you can make me clean'" (Mark 1:40). Now wouldn't it be great if we could go to the doctor today and say these same words and be cured of any disease that affects us. What a great way to practice medicine and what a wonderful health-care system we would have.

But that's not quite how it works, is it? At least not for most of us. I am leaving the door open for miraculous healings, but as a physician, miraculous healings are not what I see happen day in and day out.

Now you might say that as the doctor I don't really have the will, but I think I do. Just imagine what a great doctor I would be if it were all just a matter of willpower. If I could just will my patients to get better and they did, I would certainly do it. Everyone would love me, and I could do so much good.

Instead, in matters of healing, I often run into another source of will that I am hard pressed to understand. An example is Martha. It was almost ten years ago when Martha first came to see me as a patient, but I still think of her from time to time. She was in her early forties and had developed a sore on her breast that would not heal. There was also a hard lump underneath the sore.

I knew immediately what it was and confirmed Martha's worst fears. She had breast cancer. I reviewed with her the treatment options, but she needed time to think. "I want to go back and talk it over with my preacher and my church before I decide what to do."

I tried to reassure her. "Whatever you decide, I'll stick with you."

A week later Martha came back and told me, "I've discussed it with my church and we've decided to claim God's healing. This is God's will and if he is calling me home, I'm ready to go. I'm in his hands now."

I was shocked by her answer. She wanted no surgery, no radiation, no chemotherapy, only the healing balm of her faith in God. That alone would suffice.

For the next year I saw Martha weekly, primarily to change the bandages on her ever-growing wound. She often talked with me about her faith and her struggle to believe, but she never doubted that what was happening was God's will. One night the tumor began to bleed and would not stop. Martha died.

As disturbing as Martha's unquestioning belief in her ability to know God's will is for me, there is a side of today's practice of medicine that is equally unsettling for me.

I promise I am not making this up; it actually happened to me when I was a medical student. While on rounds one morning, my group of students presented our patients to an attending physician in our usual proficient manner. Yet when another student discussed her patient, she told of how fond she had become of the patient and included in her presentation personal likes and interests of the patient.

In a very direct manner, the attending physician interrupted her presentation saying, "Ms. Robbins, I think you are forgetting your objectivity with this patient. You are becoming too familiar with her, and it will cloud your judgment. You must learn to maintain your distance."

I knew it was wrong then, and after twenty years of being a physician, I really know it is wrong now. No one has to be taught how to be distant from another human being. That comes naturally. We all do that very well. What has to be taught is how you come close to another person, another child of God. Doing that, for most of us, is not so easy.

Throughout the New Testament, the disciples of Jesus are called upon to heal the sick. So how is the church in today's world supposed to bind up the wounds of broken bodies? Is there a middle ground between relying on our perception of God's will and capitulating to the gods of science? Surely there is.

The search for that answer is what the Church Health Center is all about. Since 1987, in midtown Memphis we have provided affordable health care to the working poor. We care for those who work to make our lives comfortable. We currently have thirty-five thousand patients who are aided by more than four hundred volunteer physicians and hundreds more dentists, nurses, and lay volunteers. The financial support comes from the faith community. We receive no government grants. This work continues to grow through the Hope and Healing Center, which seeks to help create effective, inexpensive health ministries in congregations by addressing real-life needs of the congregations.

Annie's story illustrates the ways the Church Health Center has tried to take seriously the gospel's call to a healing ministry.

Annie grew up in Mississippi, and as a child she picked cotton. But when I met her, she was working as a housekeeper here in Memphis. She had never had a doctor of her own. Annie was not well-educated, but she possessed a simple, essential dignity that never failed her. For a while, the problems that brought her to the health center were routine, but one day she showed up with a black eye. "Who did this, Annie?" I asked.

She looked at the floor. "I guess Robert got a little mad."

This was the first of many times I would see Annie after Robert physically abused her. Once I told her, "I hope I never meet him, Annie. I don't know what I'd do."

She replied, "My Jesus will take care of me, but Robert only has me to look out for him. Plus, I like you so much, I told Robert about you and I believe he's your next patient." Annie was correct, and so Robert came into my life. As you can imagine, he had a lot of problems, including drug abuse. As frequently happens with drug abusers, Robert was HIV positive.

Early on I discovered a lump in Annie's breast, which proved to be cancer. A volunteer surgeon treated Annie, and she was grateful. She only missed one week of singing in her church choir.

One day Annie came to the clinic with a sore throat. She had thrush, an unusual problem for an adult, except in one circumstance: AIDS. When Robert found out that Annie had AIDS, he left her because, he said, "After all, she's only half a woman." He was referring to her mastectomy. He conveniently forgot that Annie undoubtedly contracted the AIDS virus from him.

Annie was left alone to care for her granddaughter, Nora. Annie had custody because Nora's mother had a drug problem.

Annie did the best she could until one day she fell in the shower and broke her hip. The cancer had come back into her bones. From that day on, she never walked again. That following August, our pastoral counselor visited Annie and was disturbed to find that her only fan was broken. I told Annie's story to a kind woman who gave me a check for $500 to buy Annie an air conditioner. When the counselor took Annie the check, she graciously replied, "I only need a fan. I'd be pleased to accept the fan, but why don't you give the rest of the money to someone who needs it more than me." That is what we did.

A few weeks later, Annie's daughter called to tell me that Annie had died in her sleep. There was now only me left to take care of Robert. I continued to be his doctor for another two years until he died from complications of AIDS.

Annie exemplifies for me the triumph of the human spirit. She never shirked her responsibility to those whom she thought God had put in her care, and she never questioned that God would care for her. She never asked me for anything except to take care of Robert.

I thought the story was over, until recently when I walked into an exam room and a young girl sprang up and said, "I bet you don't know who I am." Of course I didn't have a clue. She went on, "My name is Nora, and my grandmother told me if I was ever in trouble, I could come here and you would take care of me."

And so the story goes on.

When the leper came to Jesus, the leper said, "If you will, you can make me clean." Between the leper asking and Jesus saying,

"I will," we are told that Jesus was "moved with pity" (Mark 1:41). He was moved with compassion. That is the part that is often missing in the church today.

What does it mean for us to have compassion? Although Annie's story is a powerful witness to the work of the Church Health Center and the faith community, there are a number of serious problems.

Do you believe that I am the only one who knew that Robert was abusing Annie? Can you tell me that no one in the church even suspected? And if we think that spouse abuse is not going on in the church today, then we are fooling ourselves.

Why is it that we can never say the word *breast* in church? Why didn't Annie learn about breast self-exam and mammograms in her church? God has given us a precious gift of this body and we must learn to care for it, to cherish it, and to teach our children how to nurture it and protect it from disease and keep it strong if we want to be faithful disciples.

Yet in Annie's case, that never happened. And then when Annie developed AIDS, the worst thing in the world, from her viewpoint, happened to her: From that point on, no one ever touched her. We may not be able to cure disease, but in the church we should at least be good at holding those whose bodies are broken and in pain. Yet all too often, as was the case with Annie, we wait until they die and then we all go to the funeral and shed our tears for the loss. We cannot allow this to continue to be the way the church deals with sickness and disease.

If we in the church want to take seriously the healing ministry that Christ has set before us, then it is time for us to be moved with pity. It is time for compassion to lead us in our view of our neighbor's ills. It is time for us to be moved with pity so that we can act out of love for this body, this great gift that God has given us. It is time for us to be moved with pity to draw near to the blood and sinew that we would rather someone else take care of. We must claim whatever is the leprosy of our day as our own flesh and seek to find the balm in Gilead that will heal all broken souls.

I cannot believe that it was God's will for Martha to suffer and die. Nor do I seem to have the power in my own will to say the word and watch people be cleansed of their leprosy. But we, as a community of faith, can be moved with pity, be clothed with compassion to treat Annie's body and our bodies as sacred gifts, which are bound tightly to our spirits. And if we do so, who knows what healing may occur? If you choose to follow Jesus, you cannot ignore his command to heal the sick. The only question is, Do you have the will to stand with the leper and seek the healing words that come from the Lord?

G. Scott Morris is a physician and ordained United Methodist minister. He is the founder and executive director of the Church Health Center in Memphis, Tennessee, the largest faith-based clinic for the working uninsured in America. He is also the associate pastor of St. John's United Methodist Church in Memphis.

—— 5. ——
The Healing Power of Community

MICAH D. GREENSTEIN

At camp one summer, I heard the following story attributed to Rabbi Harold Kushner: A mother sends her twelve-year-old son out on an errand and it takes him a long time to come home. When he finally gets back, the mother says, "Where were you? I was worried about you." The son says, "Oh, there's this little kid down the street whose tricycle broke and he was crying 'cause he couldn't fix it. And I really felt bad for him so I stopped to help." The mother said, "Are you trying to tell me that you know how to fix a tricycle?" And the son replies, "Of course not, Mom. I sat down and helped him cry."

There is no better way to capture the healing power of community in Judaism than the wisdom shared by the boy in this story. When the body breaks down, when forces beyond one's control cause pain and loss, when you can't fix whatever it is that's broken, you can always sit down and help someone else cry. The alternative is to leave that person crying all alone. The notion of healing in Judaism is more about presence and consolation than prayer and explanation. People whose bodies and spirits are broken do not need "answers" in times of distress. They can benefit much more from the healing power of community, whether "community" takes the form of a friend's arm around the shoulder, a prayer circle of ten (known in Judaism as a "minyan"), or an entire congregation reaching out to help.

Rabbi Nachman of Bratslav, an early Hasidic leader famous for his mystical tales, taught that a person reaches in three directions: inward to oneself, upward to God, and outward to others. The miracle of life, he taught, is that in truly reaching in any one direction, "one embraces all three." Reaching inward and upward is what Jewish prayer is largely about, and while the healing power of prayer is a core Jewish belief, so too is the healing power of community.

Two nights before I became senior rabbi of Temple Israel in Memphis, a member of the congregation committed suicide. When I arrived to meet his wife at the apartment, the family, all Russian immigrants, were understandably in shock. I stayed with them late into the night, listening to this small Russian family feeling bereft of hope.

At the funeral the next day, however, something remarkable happened. Virtually every Russian immigrant to the Memphis Jewish community showed up at the cemetery to support this tiny family! There were so many Russian speakers in the crowd, I asked a bilingual friend to stand with me as I delivered the eulogy and translate the words into Russian. The shared emotion and sense of support that the immigrant community provided this surviving family was more helpful and healing than any words I could possibly offer. The Jewish teaching that "human beings are God's language" rang true as I witnessed throngs of people bring comfort to this Russian family simply by the power of their presence.

Unique to Jewish prayer is the use of the first-person plural instead of the first-person singular. Virtually all the Hebrew prayers begin with "we" instead of "I," thus linking every individual to the larger community. This general rule holds with healing prayers too. Judaism may be the only faith that mandates that when we pray for the healing of one person, we also include all others who are ill! The prescribed prayer for healing known as the *mishebeirach lacholim* not only names the person to be healed but also prays that this person be healed, *b'toch sh'ar cholei yisrael v'chol ha'olam,* "along with all others who are in need of healing." It's as if Judaism is saying, "You are not alone in your pain and confusion. You are not isolated in your suffering. You are part of a caring community, and we are still a part of you, including those of us who share your need for physical and spiritual renewal."

Early rabbinic literature understood the truth many of us are just discovering: there are multiple dimensions to the experience of illness and healing, and each dimension affects the others. The traditional Jewish prayer for healing, for instance, speaks of healing of *nefesh* (the soul, spirit, or whole person) and healing of *guf* (body). It is not just that the state of our bodies affects the state of our souls. The reverse is just as powerful. The state of our souls affects the state of our bodies too. We can elevate the souls of others, and thereby affect their recovery, by tending to their spirits as well as their physical ailments. The paradox of healing in the Jewish tradition, therefore, is that *spiritual* healing is achieved by the *physical* presence of other human beings.

Perhaps Judaism's greatest contribution to healing, and to the human condition in general, is the primacy of community. Rabbi Wayne Dosick, author of *Soul Judaism: Dancing with God into a New Era*, sums it up well. "In community," Dosick writes, "there is shared memory, unity of purpose, mutual commitment, reciprocal responsibility, and common destiny. In community, there is powerful energy that heightens awareness, enhances prayer, and affirms transcendent experience. In community, there is sharing of tragedy amid triumph—joy enhanced, sorrow eased. In community, there is support for personal healing—the pain and sufferings of physical disease and emotional trauma tempered and soothed. In community, there is even encouragement and energy for global healing—the task of transforming and perfecting the world."[1]

We are born into community, we live in community, we learn to love and laugh with others in community. But let us not forget, as Judaism teaches, the power of community in the healing of our bodies and souls.

Note

1. Wayne Dosick, *Soul Judaism: Dancing with God into a New Era* (Woodstock, Vt.: Jewish Lights Publishing, 1999), 14.

MICAH D. GREENSTEIN is the senior rabbi of Temple Israel in Memphis, Tennessee, one of the largest Jewish congregations in the United States. Rabbi Greenstein is a leader in the Reformed Movement and teaches at Memphis Theological Seminary.

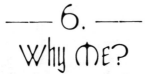

6.
Why Me?

KATHY BLACK

I t was a wonderful dance. A celebration to end four years of high school. He was with his girlfriend and they were double dating with his football buddy. Life was really good. Graduation was just around the corner. After the prom, they were going to the beach, but it started to rain.

They were in the car on the freeway deciding what to do when someone cut in front of them and forced them off the side of the road. The car hit the cement barrier, spun around, and flipped over.

The young couple in the back seat dressed in their prom finery were killed. The couple in the front seat were rushed to the hospital in critical condition. The parents of the driver arrived. Later their minister arrived, and his father wanted to know, "Why did God do this to my son?"

A divorced mother with three children who has struggled to provide for her children is diagnosed with breast cancer and she wants to know, "How much more testing is God going to require of me?"

Her twenty-first birthday was supposed to be a major milestone and celebration in her life. Instead, she buried her favorite brother—a talented actor—who died of HIV/AIDS. And shortly thereafter, she was diagnosed with schizophrenia. She has a deep and active faith and she wants to know, "Will my faith be enough to cure me?"

Girl Scout troops and Brownie troops from all over the town gathered every summer for camp at this lake. We took swimming lessons and got our swimming badges. The older scouts got their lifesaving certificates. Little did we know that the lake we swam in collected the runoff from a toxic-waste dump.

Years later, the former Girl Scouts develop cancers, brain tumors, infertility, and other strange disorders that cannot be officially diagnosed: *"damage to the autonomic nervous system due to toxic exposure."* That was my final diagnosis after two decades of tests at some of the best research hospitals in the country.

And the people of the town where the Girl Scout Camp was— a town that was begun as a Methodist Camp Meeting—want to know, "Why did God allow this to happen to our town?"

My own disability that was a result of this toxic exposure manifests itself in what I call "spells." For me, a "spell" means I lose all muscle tone and basically become paralyzed. I can hear and feel but I can't move, open my eyes, or speak.

Recently I had a "spell" in a grocery store. A half gallon of milk had fallen out of the front section of the grocery cart and was pouring out all over the floor. I bent down to set it aright and the bending over caused me to get dizzy, and I slumped to the floor.

There I was, sitting in a puddle of milk, leaning up against the celery in the produce department, unable to move, and fearful that I would fall over and hit my head on the floor, and I heard two women talking. One said to the other, "There but for the grace of God go I."

I'm sure you have your own stories about persons you know who have been diagnosed with serious diseases or who have been born with a disability or who developed a disability later in life because of an accident or illness.

You've heard the well-intended comments: "I know you have the tenacity to pass this test God has given you," or, "I'm sure God will heal you—you have such a deep faith." Or, maybe you've heard the not so well-intended comments like: "If you just had enough faith you would be cured," or, "You deserve what's happened to you."

Or maybe you've asked the question for yourself: "Why me?" "Why did God do this to me?"

All of these questions and comments imply certain things about God. That God intentionally caused the accident or illness or disability to happen. That if we just have enough faith, we will be cured. That cure seems to be the only sign that we have "passed God's test." That we deserve whatever God gives us because we have sinned and that persons with good health are blessed by God, and persons with poor health or persons with disabilities are cursed by God.

Now I realize that all these implications about God's role in relationship to illness and disability can be found in the Bible. After all, didn't Jesus say to Bartimaeus: "Your faith has made you whole"? And didn't Jesus say to the man who was paralyzed, and lowered through the roof of the house: "Your sins are forgiven"? And doesn't 1 Corinthians 10:13 say that God tests us, but that God will not test us beyond our strength?

We have inherited the biblical tradition passed down to us throughout the ages. And the popular theology we have inherited is that God is some great puppeteer in the sky who is responsible for everything. And if God doesn't intentionally cause bad things to happen to good people, God at least sits back and allows them to happen. We have been taught to believe that somehow, illness and disability are the "will of God."

But what about the other biblical witnesses? In John 9 when Jesus and his disciples encounter a man born blind, Jesus says to the disciples: "Neither this man nor his parents sinned" (v. 3). And what *about* the man who was paralyzed and lowered through the roof of a house? Jesus praises the faith of the four *friends* who brought him to Jesus, not the faith of the man.

And when Jesus comes down from the mountain after the transfiguration, Jesus chastises the *disciples* for their lack of faith, not the faithlessness of the father or the boy living with severe convulsions.

And though Jesus did say to the one person with leprosy who returned to give thanks that his faith made him well, the other nine were also cured of their leprosy with no mention of their faith, or lack thereof.

And the word faith is not found at all in the stories in which Jesus cured the leper in Matthew 8 or the Syrophoenician woman's daughter or the man who was deaf in Mark 7. Faith is not found in the story of the man who was blind from Bethsaida in Mark 8 or the man named "Legion" who lived in the tombs in Luke 8 or the woman who had been bent over for eighteen years in Luke 13 or numerous other stories.

And while we have many stories in the Bible of the people Jesus cured, there are thousands more who did not receive a cure. And isn't *that* what we struggle with today? Not only the question "Why me?" "Why did God do this to me?" But also, "Why not me?" "Why am I not one of the chosen few to receive a miracle, a cure?"

Somewhere along the line, Christians have received a message that if we are faithful, we will have health, wealth, and happiness. We deserve it as a reward for being a good Christian.

But this message denies the other biblical witness that talks about the cost of discipleship, the thorn in the flesh, the limp we get when we wrestle with God's angel, the suffering and persecution that we will experience for the sake of the gospel.

And the truth is *bad things do happen to good people*. And people who sell drugs, commit murder, or abuse children are often in excellent health.

So how do we reconcile the biblical witnesses and what we've been taught about God with our own experience of health and ill-health?

First, I want to say that I don't believe God had anything to do with causing my disability. To believe that, I would have to believe that God caused a person to earn a living by collecting toxic waste, letting the canisters rust so that the toxins leaked into two stream beds that flowed into the lake. Then God guided the Girl Scout leaders to choose this lake for their camp. Then God urged my parents to send me and my sisters to the camp and later urged me to become a lifeguard for Brownie camp—*all* so that I could get this particular disability. This is not the kind of God in whom I can believe. It sounds more like a monster out of a Hollywood horror picture.

Accidents happen. The factories that make the products we buy pollute our air and water. Germs and diseases emerge and mutate. Chemicals in our brain become imbalanced. Our genes pass on both dominant and recessive traits that may show up as diseases or disabilities in future generations depending on who our offspring marry. Sometimes we can control things by the choices we make, and sometimes we have no control over what happens to us. Given the pollution in our world, the number of car accidents, airplane accidents, and sports accidents that happen every year, maybe the question should be, "Why *not* me?"

Illness, disease, and disability happen. I do not believe that God is the great puppeteer in the sky making decisions about who gets cancer and who becomes blind. I do believe that God is with us at every moment of our lives, loving us and cradling us, as we cope with the many trials we face on life's journey. God is there to give us the strength to channel our *anger* about our condition in positive ways. God is there to help us move out of feeling sorry for ourselves so that we can get on with our lives. God is there to change our victim status to survivor status.

Sure, we learn many lessons, and our faith may be strengthened *because* of our illness or disability, or, *in spite of it*. But that does not mean that God caused someone to be born deaf *in order to learn* these lessons.

But when something does happen, God is there, offering us opportunities for healing and transformation at every moment of our lives.

One of the confusing things about our biblical heritage is this notion of *healing*. We tend to equate the word *healing* with *cure*. We say "Jesus *healed* Bartimaeus," but what we really mean is, "Jesus *cured* Bartimaeus."

But in the English language, there is a difference between *healing* and *cure*. Healing has many meanings: a healing moment, a healing presence, a healing relationship, a healing touch.

Jesus' ministry was truly about healing—not just cure. Jesus touched the man with leprosy, Jesus singled out Bartimaeus from the crowd, Jesus called the woman with the hemorrhage "daughter."

With each touch, Jesus would have been considered "unclean" himself according to the Jewish purity codes. Yet Jesus broke the rules in order to bring people back into relationship with other people, to bring individuals back into community. *That* is what healing is all about: being accepted for who you are, having a sense of belonging to a community, being in relationship with others.

Too often, however, illness and disability separate people from their faith community, from important relationships in their lives.

Each of us, those with disabilities and those without, is called to make choices at every moment of our lives that will facilitate healing in the lives of ourselves and others. We may pray for a cure for those who live with illnesses that may be curable. We may pray for a cure for those who live with permanent disabilities. There is always hope.

But in the meantime, it is crucial that we focus on *healing* rather than *cure;* that we love and accept people for who they are, and not imply that they are only acceptable and worthy of full participation *if* they are cured.

If we believe God caused the illness or disability, then we feel we are justified to separate out, to push aside those we feel God is punishing, or testing, to turn away those we believe do not have enough faith. They become "unclean" in our day.

But, if we understand that rather than *causing* the illness or disability, God accepts us and is supporting us, nurturing us, bringing healing into our lives at every moment, then Christians can likewise accept, support, and nurture those who are not cured.

We can be God's agents of healing in our hurting world.

KATHY BLACK is professor of homiletics and liturgics at Claremont School of Theology in Claremont, California. She is an ordained United Methodist minister and a pioneer in preaching in the deaf community. Her two most recent books are *Culturally Conscious Worship* and *A Healing Homiletic: Preaching and Disability.*

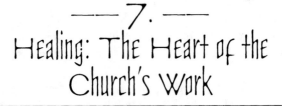

—— 7. ——
Healing: The Heart of the Church's Work

John 9:1-11

JAMES A. FORBES JR.

I t should not have been a surprise to the disciples that day when Jesus rebuked them for misunderstanding what his special concern was. It was the day when they passed a blind man on the road and Jesus stopped and gazed at that man and looked deeply into his sockets where his eyes were to be. The disciples assumed that Jesus was concerned about the source of this man's challenge. "Who sinned," they asked Jesus, "this man or his parents, that he was born blind?" (John 9:2). Jesus was annoyed that they should ask that question because it reflected what is all too common. People are so eager to get into the blame and shame game. It is almost as if they, his own disciples, assumed that the heart of the work of ministry was searching out transgressors or identifying the cause of some shortcoming. Of course, the gospel is always concerned about morality. The gospel is concerned to help people develop good character traits. But some people think that church is primarily about checking folks out, checking them twice so that we can find out who's naughty or nice, so we can condemn somebody. If that's your understanding, Jesus seems to be saying to the disciples, I have worked with you all three years and you still don't know what is at the heart of my concern. He rebuked them when he said, "Neither this man nor his parents sinned" (John 9:3), not suggesting they were sinless, but suggesting that is not the point. The issue is that this man's condition

39

represents an opportunity for the work of God to be done. I am not searching out some kind of far-off generational experience that has doomed this man to blindness. I'm just circling around him in order that I can find a place where the healing can begin in this man.

The reason I say the disciples should not have been surprised is that they had been with Jesus for three years in a very intimate ministry. They'd been with him day by day. They had left their homes to follow him. Had they not heard him that first day when he stood up and said, "The Spirit of the Lord is upon me, because he has anointed me to bring good news to the poor. He has sent me to proclaim release to the captives and recovery of sight to the blind, to let the oppressed go free, to proclaim the year of the Lord's favor" (Luke 4:18-19)? Had they not heard him talk about how God had healed Naaman, a Syrian (Luke 4:27)? How the Syrophoenician woman had been healed by God (Matt. 15:21; Mark 7:25-30)? Had they missed out on it? Had they forgotten that when Jesus called them and gave them their briefing for their discipleship, he said, "Proclaim the good news, 'The kingdom of heaven has come near.' Cure the sick, raise the dead, cleanse the lepers, cast out demons" (Matt. 10:7-8)? Had they forgotten that Jesus, even after preaching in Capernaum, had immediately gone to Peter's house where his mother-in-law lay ill with a fever, and Jesus, at the very beginning of his ministry, had lifted her up and the fever had departed (Mark 1:29-31)? Had they forgotten that that very same afternoon when Jesus had just gotten his ministry started, that after this woman had been healed, people from all over the community brought their sick and lay them at the door and there was a healing service like they had never seen before (Mark 1:32-34)?

Take out the healing stories from the gospel and you've got pretty much a skeleton of a story left. For Jesus' ministry was preaching, teaching, and healing. They were there at the very center of his ministry. The woman with the issue of blood; the paralytic brought in and let down on a sheet in front of Jesus; the man with the withered hand; the woman bent over; and the sick child lying at the point of death, with her mother, the

Syrophoenician woman, saying, "Please help my daughter." I mean, have the disciples forgotten about the Gerasene demoniac, crazy in the hills crying out? Jesus comes by and brings peace to his mind.

Had they forgotten even the one event that really should have made it clear to them that healing was to be at the heart of their ministry? After Jesus left the mountain after his transfiguration, he came down from the mountain with Peter, James, and John following him, and they were surprised when they found the scribes were arguing with the other disciples (Mark 9:14-29). And let me tell you what they were arguing about. They were arguing about the fact that a man had brought his son to Jesus. And Jesus was not there. And the man said, "Nevertheless, you are his disciples. He has charged you to be healers." They were arguing with the disciples. "You say you are the disciples of Christ. You say Christ is the Messiah. You say Jesus is the holy one who is to come. Why can't you heal this brother who has this demon situation?" When Jesus came down they were arguing. And Jesus, at that point, had said to them, "Oh faithless generation. How long must I be with you before you come to understand that healing is at the heart of this ministry? That you are called upon to watch me. See what I do. Notice how I put my hand in the ears of the one who cannot hear and then I touch their tongue so they can speak again. Notice how I find those persons who are at the point of death and by the power that is in me, they are healed and presented back to their parents again. Oh faithless generation," he said. "How long must I be with you? Bring the boy to me." And they saw Jesus heal that boy, raise him up again. After that, they were disciples and they wanted to be briefed on what they had seen. They got into the house, and because they didn't want the crowd to see and to hear, they waited until after everybody else was gone, then they asked Jesus, "Tell us, why could we not cast that demon out?" (Mark 9:28).

Jesus answered them simply, "This kind of power only comes through prayer" (Mark 9:29). Of course the King James Version adds "prayer and fasting."

We have become experts here at referring people to other places to get healed. Because you wouldn't expect a church like this, with its Gothic architecture, with its stained-glass windows, with pew upon pew to be involved in a serious ministry of healing. We can have good singing and pretty good preaching, but if anybody is sick we have a register of the best physicians we can refer you to. In fact, I have a whole list of hospitals we could send you to: Beth Israel, Charity Health System, Catholic Hospital Center, Columbia Presbyterian Center, Episcopal Health Service, or St. John's Episcopal Hospital. I've got a lot of saints listed here—Lutheran, Methodist Center, Nmonedes, Mount Sinai, St. Luke's. As I got to reading this list, I started wondering why all these saints are listed with these hospitals. Because people need to know that the church has as one of its primary ministries healing the people. In fact, the church was the first hospital. The church, even in the Middle Ages, knew that if nobody else cared for those who did not have care, it was the responsibility of the church to be a healing center. Do you get my point?

But now we have been blessed with this beautiful edifice, and we are a high-class church, and we have some of the most upwardly mobile citizens of the world who are regularly a part this interfaith, interdenominational, international church. I am afraid that if we don't embrace the healing ministry, we will be condemned along with the disciples. And Jesus says to them, "I am not so much worried about finding out the source of the sin that led to the illness. In fact it is faulty theology to say that every time somebody is ill it is because of somebody's sin. I am here and the reason I was looking at the brother so hard was because I recognized that this is likely to be the last time I pass this way. He has been sitting there as we come in and out of the community. We have thrown him a pence or two as we pass by, but if I miss him this time, it may be the last time. And furthermore, I need to see this man through if only to reveal to you that I am in the world. And as long as I am in the world I am the Light of the world. But night is coming."

This was his way of talking about his crucifixion. This is his way of saying, "I won't be here much longer. And if I cannot transfer to you a sense of the importance and the centrality of healing, I will return to my heavenly parent and my disciples will forget what my mission was all about." Whereupon he lectured and then he stooped down.

I think when I preached this sermon last time I violated some of the canons of propriety because I remember I came down and spat on the floor and made some mud and put it on the man's eyes. Although I will not do that again, let me suggest to you that what happened was that Jesus made spittle and mud and put it on the eyes of the man and said, "Go, wash in the pool of Siloam" (John 9:7). And the man went and came back, and he was able to see.

This year what I want to emphasize is that if the disciples had never allowed it to sink in, when Jesus said to them, "We must work the work of Him that sent me; I came to heal and you, my disciples, are called upon to be healers as well."

May I pause now? I'd like to see the hand of everyone who considers himself or herself to be a disciple of the Christ. That is, if you consider yourself to be a Christian. Let me see your hands. But please, as you raise it, I want you to hold it there just a moment because from what I read in this text, all these hands I see are called upon to be healing hands. These hands are healing hands! Jesus intends that our hands will heal. And if we haven't been aware of it, then thank God, health day has come along. Because this is a time to remind us all that we have a ministry of healing. I want to suggest to you today that if we begin to accept this vocation of healing, then perhaps the world in which we live will be able to hold off the impulses that lead to war, and we may find ourselves coming closer to the day when peace prevails in our community. When war comes "down by the riverside, we can put our swords and our shields away, down by the riverside." Because we will have become a center of healing.

Now some of you may ask, "How is this so?" First, I would suggest to you that when Jesus said he was healing, it was because the spirit of the Lord God was upon him. You have heard me say a lot in the last year that I look forward to the spiritual revitalization of the nation. That is to say that when the power of the Holy

Spirit releases the gifts of healing that are in us. This is why I continue to explore what it means for a congregation to be anointed with the Holy Spirit. I have looked at various methods by which that happens. I have thought about baptism as a sign of the anointing. I have talked about sprinkling—whether it is immersion or sprinkling. I have looked at oil—we anointed some of you with oil. Others were anointed during our Ash Wednesday service. But I think "anointing" is to pray. To pray that God's living presence will rest upon us. That every member of the church will understand that when they accepted Jesus Christ as Lord, part of the package was that the Holy Spirit was available, taking residency in our lives to release the areas that are constricted so that our hands could truly heal. That's what I am praying for. I pray for you, congregation. I pray for you when you don't even know it. And when I pray, do you know what I'm asking? "Lord, fill the Riverside Church with the power of your spirit. Lord, let the flow of your spirit create a tidal wave of love. Lord, let your spirit flow so that the people will have the impediments of their own lives somehow burned up by the fire of the spirit so that love can flow through them and so that there will be healing hands."

I pray that God will turn the whole Riverside Church into a massive altar so that wherever you sit, there are Christians near you who know that they've got healing hands. And that when we have the passing of the peace they put their hands on you and say, "May the Lord bless you," and you all of a sudden say, "I'm feeling something." What I'm suggesting is not an ancient ritual. It is a contemporary manifestation of the power of the spirit. That just by being here and by chanting, whether it is "Shalom" or "Siloam," that the chanting sound will get a certain resonance in the air and wherever that little speck is that is robbing us of the flow of God's grace, it'll move out. Do you all hear what I'm trying to say?

I would like to tell you that when Jesus talked to his disciples he showed them that healing was key. That means that healing can happen just by our touching one another.

That day when Jesus sent that man to the pool of Siloam, he involved several methods. One was that the man was sent. You can't help much if you are trying to heal somebody who does not consent. There may be some invasive forms of healing that heal you whether you want to be healed or not, but I would assume that is very rare. Somehow you have got to consent to the wholeness that is being offered. Jesus used his spittle and the clay of the earth, and I think there is a wisdom in this. We people think that bacteria is a bad thing, little knowing that is where we all came from. A batch of bacteria stirred up in the right proportions with divine grace. That's where life came from. So Jesus used a little bacteria, mixed it up just right, to help the regenerative process where the eyes ought to be.

Then notice that the disciples were expected to go and help in the healing process. It was as they healed together that all of the methods seemed to work together. Whatever it takes to bring us to health and wholeness, that is what God sends.

JAMES A. FORBES JR. is the senior minister at Riverside Church in New York City. He was recognized by *Newsweek* magazine in 1996 as one of the twelve most effective preachers in the English-speaking world.

— 8. —
Arthritis of the Spirit

Matthew 18:21-22

BARBARA BROWN TAYLOR

I n case you have not noticed, Christianity is a religion in which the sinners have all the advantages. They can step on your feet fifty times and you are supposed to keep smiling. They can talk bad about you every time you leave the room and it is your job to excuse them with no thought of getting even. The burden is on you, because you have been forgiven yourself, and God expects you to do unto others as God has done unto you.

This is not a bad motivation for learning how to forgive. If God is willing to stay with me in spite of my meanness, my weakness, my stubborn self-righteousness, then who am I to hold those same things against someone else? Better I should confess my own sins than keep track of yours, only it is hard to stay focused on my shortcomings. I would so much rather stay focused on yours, especially when they are hurtful to me.

Staying angry with you is how I protect myself from you. Refusing to forgive you is not only how I punish you; it is also how I keep you from getting close enough to hurt me again, and nine times out of ten it works, only there is a serious side effect. It is called bitterness, and it can do terrible things to the human body and soul.

Last week on a trip into Atlanta I stopped at a gift shop to buy a couple of wedding presents, some nice brass picture frames, which I asked the clerk to wrap. "Well, who are they for?" she snarled. "Are you going to tell me or am I supposed to guess?" I looked at her then for the first time and saw a heavy, middle-aged woman whose brow was all bunched up over two hard, cold eyes. Her mouth turned down at the sides like she had just tasted something rancid and she had both her hands planted on the glass counter, leaning against it with such malice that I thought she might push it over on me if I irritated her any further.

Generally speaking, I get mad when someone comes at me like that, but this time I just got scared, because I could see what her anger had done to her and I wanted to get away from it before it did something similar to me. Actually, it was something stronger than plain anger that had twisted that woman's face. All by itself, anger is not that damaging. It is not much more than that quick rush of adrenaline you feel when you are being threatened. It tells you that something you hold dear is in danger—your property, your beliefs, your physical safety. I think of anger as a kind of flashing yellow light. "Caution," it says, "something is going on here. Slow down and see if you can figure out what it is."

When I do slow down, I can usually learn something from my anger, and if I am lucky I can use the energy of it to push for change in myself or in my relationships with others. Often I can see my own part in what I am angry about, and that helps, because if I had a hand in it then I can concentrate on getting my hand back out of it again instead of spinning my wheels in blame. I can, in other words, figure out what my anger has to teach me and then let it go, but when my anger goes on and on without my learning or changing anything then it is not plain anger anymore. It has become bitterness instead. It has become resentment, which a friend of mine calls "arthritis of the spirit."

So there is another motivation for learning how to forgive—not only because we owe it to God but because we owe it to ourselves. Because resentment deforms us. Because unforgiveness is a boomerang. We use it to protect ourselves—to hurt back before we can be hurt again—but it has a sinister way of circling right back at us so that we become the victims of our own ill will.

One summer the *New York Times Book Review* ran a series on the deadly sins. Joyce Carol Oates wrote on despair, Gore Vidal wrote on pride, and John Updike, of all people, wrote on lust. Mary Gordon's essay on anger was a real beauty, chiefly because she was willing to admit she knew a lot about it. One hot August afternoon, she wrote, she was in the kitchen preparing dinner for ten. Although the house was full of people, no one offered to help her chop, stir, or set the table. She was stewing in her own juices, she said, when her seventy-eight-year-old mother and her two small children insisted that she stop what she was doing and take them swimming.

They positioned themselves in the car, she said, leaning on the horn and shouting her name out of the window so all the neighbors could hear them, loudly reminding her that she had promised to take them to the pond. That, Gordon said, was when she lost it. She flew outside and jumped on the hood of the car. She pounded on the windshield. She told her mother and her children that she was never, ever going to take any of them anywhere and none of them was ever going to have one friend in any house of hers until the hour of their death—which, she said, she hoped was soon.

Then the frightening thing happened. "I became a huge bird," she said. "A carrion crow. My legs became hard stalks, my eyes were sharp and vicious. I developed a murderous beak. Greasy black feathers took the place of arms. I flapped and flapped. I blotted out the sun's light with my flapping." Even after she had been forced off the hood of the car, she said, it took her a while to come back to herself and when she did she was appalled, because she realized she had genuinely frightened her children. Her son said to her, "I was scared because I didn't know who you were."

"Sin makes the sinner unrecognizable," Gordon concluded, and the only antidote to it is forgiveness, but the problem is that anger is so exciting, so enlivening, that forgiveness can seem like a limp surrender. If you have ever cherished a resentment, you know how right it can make you feel to have someone in the world whom you believe is all wrong. You may not be up to admitting it yet, but one of the great benefits of having an enemy is that you get to look good by comparison. It also helps to have someone to blame for why your life is not turning out the way it was supposed to.

Last Friday on National Public Radio I heard Linda Wirtheimer talking to a correspondent in the Middle East about the amazing things that are happening there between Israelis and Palestinians. "How are people reacting?" she asked him. "After all, losing an enemy is as upsetting as losing a friend." I hadn't thought about it that way before, but she is right. When you allow your enemy to stop being your enemy, all the rules change. Nobody knows how to act anymore, because forgiveness is an act of transformation. It does not offer the adrenaline rush of anger, nor the feeling of power that comes from a well-established resentment. It is a quiet revolution, as easy to miss as a fist uncurling to become an open hand, but it changes people in ways that anger only wishes it could.

So why don't we do it more often? Because it is scary, to lay down your arms like that, to trade in your pride and your power on the off-chance that you may discover something more valuable than either of them. "To forgive," writes Mary Gordon, "is to give up the exhilaration of one's own unassailable rightness." And there is loss in that, only it is the loss of an illusion, and what is gained is unmistakably real: the chance to live again, free from the bitterness that draws the sweetness from our lives, that gives us scary faces and turns us into carrion crows who blot out the sun with our flapping. No one else does this to us. We do it to ourselves, but we do not have to.

We are being forgiven every day of our lives. We are being set free by someone who has arranged things so that we have all the advantages. We have choices. We have will. And we have an advocate, who seems to know that we need lots of practice at this forgiveness business. How often should we forgive? Will seven times take care of it? "Not seven times," Jesus said, "but, I tell you, seventy-seven times." This is no chore. This is a promise, because forgiveness is the way of life. It is God's cure for the deformity our resentments cause us. It is how we discover our true shape, and every time we do it we get to be a little more alive. What God knows and we don't yet is that once we get the hang of it, seventy times seven won't be enough, not to mention seventy-seven.

We'll be so carried away by it that we'll hope it never ends.

BARBARA BROWN TAYLOR is an Episcopal priest who teaches religion at Piedmont College in rural northeast Georgia. Before becoming a full-time teacher in 1997, she spent fifteen years in parish ministry. In 2001, she joined the faculty of Columbia Theological Seminary in Decatur, Georgia, as adjunct professor of spirituality. Her most recent books are *Speaking of Sin: The Lost Language of Salvation* and *The Luminous Web: Essays on Science and Religion.*

—— 9. ——
Healing

WILLIAM E. SWING

I mention to you the word healing from the pulpit and what comes to your mind? Oral Roberts? Professional healers who seem so suspect? The Christian Scientists? A place in France with crutches hanging around where lame people were made well? Jesus giving sight to a blind man? Perhaps.

While you are at the grocery store, suppose someone there mentions the word *healing*, then what comes to your mind? Doctors? Hospitals? Psychiatrists? Beds? Medicine? Perhaps.

Whatever your reaction to the word *healing*, it is pretty safe to assume that you have some thoughts on the subject. Basically it seems to be that the word *healing* is a positive word. As a child, it meant parental attention, sympathy, warmth, home and hearth. As we grow older, it means pain, chance of escalating illness, costly time, certain financial payments. Though these ambiguous connotations do get tacked onto the definition, I think that most of us react favorably to the word *healing*, although this favorable reaction shifts quickly to profound suspicion when "healing" is associated with the church.

But the church has a healing ministry. Although the church has spent several hundred embarrassed years disguising this fact, it really does have a healing ministry. No sooner do these words come out of my mouth than I sense the rising giant waves of suspicion and even hostility from most Christians. You might be wondering if the preacher has started on a wild new kick, if he is insulting doctors by presupposing that the church is interested in healing. You might be wondering if I have in mind turning the worship of the church into a magic circus of attempting to pull off miracles. And I will admit that it is quite natural to be anxious about this subject in church because of a few abuses over the years. Yet, it is time to declare that, indeed, the church has a ministry of healing.

Isn't it safe to say that the common understanding of healing holds that a man or woman should take his or her characteristic illness to the characteristic practitioner? If something is wrong with his body, he should go to a physician. If something is wrong with her spirit, she should go to a clergyperson. If something is wrong with his mind, he should go to a psychiatrist.

But then, two things must quickly be said. First, it is most important that the professional men and women stick to their vocations. A psychiatrist who acts like a priest, or a priest who acts like a doctor, or a doctor who acts like a psychiatrist is liable to do a great deal of damage and actually suffocate the healing process. It is only right for a person to do only what he or she is trained to do.

On the other hand, the human being is not so simply harmonized that one can pull out the mind and work with it, or deal only with the spirit. It's easy to forget how many physical illnesses are symptoms of emotional or spiritual maladies. It is almost impossible to isolate completely any one ingredient of a human because we seem to be an indivisible symphony of instrumental parts. Therefore, in order to deal with a person, we must deal with the whole person, and not simply one section that has been drawn and quartered for our convenience.

All that we know about the church's ministry of healing is couched in our basic understanding of the person as a whole person, as well as our understanding of the limitations of professional healers. But what exactly is the church's ministry of healing? Where did it come from? What does it mean for Christians today?

With all due respect to modern misunderstandings, the church did not get into the area of healing as a publicity stunt to enhance its public image and to attract interested potential members. As a matter of fact, the church did not even create the healing ministry; it simply fell heir to it. Jesus Christ healed first; then he gave his ministry to the church in sacred trust.

As the Scriptures say, Christ came preaching, teaching, and healing. Wherever he went, he brought life and health. He charted a straight course through life, and when we retrace his steps, viewing what he left behind, we are impressed with his ministry to the whole person. In the path that he left behind, in his earthly reign, we not only see souls healed, emancipated by the forgiveness of sins, we not only see mentalities healed and reshaped because of his teachings, but we also see people healed of their physical illnesses if they could come close enough to touch the hem of his garment.

To say that Christ was a "spiritual healer" would be to ignore him when he spit on clay and put it on a blind man's eyes or when he told ten lepers to go take a bath in the river. To say that Christ was a "physical healer" would be to ignore him when he forgave the woman taken in adultery or when he forgave the sins of the paralytic. To say that Christ was a "psychological healer" would be to ignore him when he exorcised the demons in a man called Legion. To narrow the healing ministry of Christ to the categories that we are most able to deal with seems to be an effort to "get him down to our size." But he doesn't fit into our picture. Jesus Christ was not a physician. He was not a psychiatrist. He was not a priest. Yet his ministry of healing was profoundly effective, and most important, it was directed toward a person as an integrated, whole being, not a little bit of this together with a little bit of that. He made people not only holy but whole.

This is the healing ministry that the church inherits. It is very surprising to a sophisticated mind and very humbling to a Christian to be aware that, of all the ways in which God could effect healing in the world, he chose the church to be the instrument of the healing ministry of his Son. This does not mean that other ministries of healing, which are not Christian, are disqualified or in contempt, but on the other hand, healing ministries should not discredit the church's inherited healing ministry. The church should not be haughty about its gift, but it should not hide its gift either.

As church people, all of us receive assignments to participate in this healing ministry. It is not reserved simply for church services or tent meetings or confessional booths. One physician stated that he believes each Christian has a healing ministry, with each person possessing certain talents. This healing does not have to be something extraordinary, and oftentimes it can be something as simple as showing love and care for others. It is exemplified in parents taking care of sick children, a person helping a family when a member is sick by running errands or bringing food, or praying for someone in trouble.

But in reality, what is the sense of a healing ministry like in our church? Nonexistent? Almost, I fear. That is too bad. Every time we have tried to hoist the flag of healing, we have been swamped by the rumor of abuses, by fear of being in competition with the American Medical Association, by plain old cold feet. That flag of healing has been run down. We keep it in the church like an ancient relic in a museum. We let the Sunday school teachers get it out of its case to show the children, and we tell them about how Jesus healed people—we sort of expect the children to swoon—and then quickly put it away. But that flag is out in the open now. Be it known that the church is aware of its ministry of healing and will not back away from it.

One night each week during Lent there will be healing services. Not spiritual healing, not physical healing, not psychological healing, but the healing of the whole person, the healing that Christ brings to those who reach out in faith. We will pray for those who want or who need our prayers. We will explore in greater depth what this ministry of healing is about. We will practice bringing more of ourselves to the living presence of God's spirit. We will receive the outward, visible sign of the laying on of hands and a token of the inward spiritual grace of healing.

Our Lenten healing service will not exhaust the healing ministry of the church. As a matter of fact, this Communion service today is the most eloquent healing service of all. But what we look for in the Lenten healing services is a focus that will bring our attention to what happens when we voluntarily look to God for healing. We want people to continue going to doctors and psychiatrists and counselors. We are not in competition with them. We are only trying to be true to our Lord who comes to us, preaching, teaching, and healing the whole person.

WILLIAM E. SWING is the Episcopal Bishop of California. He is the founder of the "United Religions of the World," an outgrowth of the United Nations 50th Anniversary held in San Francisco in June 2000.

— 10. —
Walk Tall

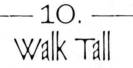

Luke 13:10-13

REGINALD MALLETT

During the summer of 1940, I used to go to the indoor public swimming pool with my school friends on Saturday mornings.

The way back to the bus stop took us beside the fish market where we used to see a little man. You could hardly miss him because even on the hottest days he wore a long raincoat that reached down to his ankles and on his head he wore a rather ridiculous looking top hat. He used to push a baby carriage in which there was a gramophone. The carriage was covered in patriotic posters announcing what would happen to Hitler and his gang and telling us to keep our chins up despite the air raids and the bombing. He appeared to be a harmless chap who played cheerful morale boosting records. He relied for a living on passersby who would take pity on him and put coins in a box that hung at the front of the carriage.

Now we children thought that we knew the truth about this man. We believed that he was a spy planted in our fish market by the Nazi High Command to undermine the British war effort. We reasoned that he was hiding his espionage under a great show of false patriotism that all his posters and music proclaimed. He did not, however, fool us. We had penetrated his secret and we *knew* that the harmless looking gramophone was really a disguised radio transmitter and that he was passing on vital information concerning activity in our fish market that would be most helpful for an enemy victory. We therefore did not shrink from striking blows for liberty by giving the baby carriage a push each time we passed it and then running away.

Of course it was all nonsense. Foolish childish ideas. The man was no more a spy than was Winston Churchill. Our wild fancies about this poor man were just figments of our childish imaginations.

Looking back, I think I know why that dear harmless man appeared so sinister to us children. He was bent almost double. To our silly childish minds he stooped because he was trying to hide his face, a sure sign of guilt. We never actually looked him in the eyes. Much later when I studied medicine, I learned about the terrible condition of Ankylosing Spondilitis and then realized what was wrong with that man. I would give much to be able to go to him now, bend down, look him in the eyes, and tell him how sorry I am that we misjudged him so. I think he would probably smile and tell me that he understood.

Here in the gospel story is a woman who has been bent double for *eighteen years*. Think of it! Eighteen years looking at the pavement. Eighteen years not being able to look up at the sun and the stars! Eighteen years of not being able to look others in the eyes. It is significant that the incident is only recorded by Luke the physician. No doubt he included the story in his narrative in order to introduce the teaching of Jesus about the keeping of regulations governing the Sabbath. It is, however, worthy of closer attention for its own sake.

WHERE HEALING TOOK PLACE— THE SYNAGOGUE

Wallace Hamilton was a much loved Methodist preacher in the United States. He told of how the pastor of a downtown church was jolted out of a mediocre ministry by a sharp question asked by a casual visitor in his congregation.

The morning was hot and stuffy and the service lacked any inspiration. The congregation was small and sleepy. From behind their waving fans they looked not too hopefully toward the pulpit where the preacher, evidently ill-prepared, struggled with his sermon and didn't do well. It was an ineffective performance.

When it was over he stood at the church door as usual to greet his congregation as they filed out. "Hot day Reverend," one man said. "Yes, dreadful," he replied. "Good morning Brother Robin," said another, "I hope it rains today." "Yes," the preacher answered, "that would be a blessing." And so one by one, the congregation said some perfunctory word as each left the church. Then suddenly he was shaking hands with a stranger. And something in the eyes and bearing of the man made the preacher uneasy. "My name is Robin," said the preacher. "Yes, I know," the stranger answered. "And you?" inquired the minister. "Only a watchman," the stranger replied. "A watchman," the minister repeated. "Yes," the man said. "Well we're glad to have you in church," the minister said. "Come again sir, come again." And then the question, a sharp stinging word, "*Why?*" The preacher didn't see any more people after that though he continued to shake hands. He no longer heard what they said as they filed out. One word drummed in his ears, "Why?" "Come again." "Why?"[1]

Is there something happening in church that will make us want to come again? I am uncomfortable with gimmicks and artificial attempts to be sensational. Worship is too awesome a business for that. But it is sad when worship is dull.

Something happened in the synagogue that day because Jesus was present. And where there is true worship He always is present and something momentous inevitably happens. Broken hearts are mended. Spiritually blind eyes see again. Hard spirits are melted. Enmities are ended. It is so easy to talk down the church, to criticize it, and to parade its shortcomings. We need to talk up the church and recall all the blessings we have received from it.

The church ought to be a therapeutic community, a place where the walking wounded come to find comfort and healing. The church ought to be a sign of the Kingdom, that the reign of God is already breaking in upon the earth. And we need to thank God for all those who come bringing their bent backs, their scarred lives, and their abject spirits and find renewal and life because Christ is there: "*His touch has still its ancient power.*"

Look out across any congregation and there will be someone there who has spondylitis in one form or another. Perhaps it is one who has damaged emotions, a victim of abuse inflicted by those who ought to have offered love. Or perhaps the problem is unconfessed and unresolved sin with a crippling burden of hideous mental images from a guilty past. Or perhaps there is one who is stooped over because of disillusionment, feeling betrayed by those who were trusted. Or again, perhaps the affliction is disappointment with all the brokenness of shattered hopes and dreams.

Will worship be for these bent persons a liberating experience as it was for the woman in the synagogue? Will they want to come again because they have been touched and made whole? Will they leave the house of God walking tall?

THE ONE TO WHOM THE HEALING CAME— THE PATIENT

It is easy to suppose that this woman was old. But was she? Ankylosing Spondilitis, although more common in men is also present in women, and it usually strikes early, when the victim is only a teenager. Perhaps this woman was just eighteen when she first became aware of the disease, and although she had been stooped over for eighteen years, she might not yet have celebrated her fortieth birthday.

Think of it! Bent double so that all she could see were feet and the ground. Not the most dignified of postures. When conquerors wanted to humiliate subjects they made them walk with their backs bowed. One of the most cruel aspects of Ankylosing Spondilitis is that the sufferer cannot walk tall.

Once this unfortunate woman had been a young girl tripping happily with her friends. Once she would have had the dreams common to maturing young women in that culture; dreams of love, home, and children of her own. Then came the illness that changed everything. There is no mention of any friends or family in the story. Was she alone? I wonder when someone last embraced her and gave her a hug to assure her of her worth? It is difficult to hug someone who is bent double. Try it sometime and see for yourself. And eighteen years is a long time to have to walk with your face to the ground.

Does anyone understand this woman as she shuffles along? There are no birds on the wing for her, only feet. No trees, only feet. No faces, only feet. No sun in the sky, only feet. No stars at night, only feet. Her world is one of shadows and gutters. I hope such a child of God will always find love and understanding in church. If worship is to be real and if preaching is to be more than just words *then it must be remembered that there are men and women in attendance at every service who are stooped over mentally, emotionally, and spiritually.*

It is significant that we meet this woman with Ankylosing Spondylitis *in the Synagogue.* I am moved whenever I see anyone who has cause to be angry with God coming to worship him. I think of two dear sisters in their sixties, Kathleen and Margaret. Kathleen was blind and lame. Margaret was deaf, stooped over, and partially sighted. And yet they never missed worship even in the fiercest of weather and their spirits were sweet and serene. They were a testimony to the grace of God.

I understand those so hurt by the bitter blows of life that they turn away from God. I understand but I am saddened. This is just the time when they need Him most. The church is the place for the broken, the hurt, the frightened, the resentful. It is for the people who are so bent by life that they cannot look up and see the sky. If calamity has come to you, if you have found yourself in that dark pit of depression or suffering don't turn your back on God. That is when you need him most. Keep the channels open to receive the wholeness that can come through the life of the spirit so that you too may be enabled to walk tall.

THE ONE FROM WHOM
THE HEALING FLOWED—JESUS

Jesus did not give this unfortunate patient advice on how to walk tall; he enabled her to do it. He had an instinct for sensing someone with need. It is shared by all who have received His spirit.

Early in my Christian experience I went one Sunday morning to hear the late Dr. W. E. Sangster at the Central Hall, Westminster. He was considered not only one of the greatest preachers in London but in the whole of England. I little dreamed that this saintly man would become my friend.

After the service, I stood in the vestibule of the Great Hall. There were two exit doors from the auditorium. I chose the one on the right and stood near a nervous little elderly lady who was obviously in distress. Clutching her handbag in one hand she wiped tears from her eyes with the other. By the second exit door a group of foreign diplomats also stood waiting. I found myself contrasting their elegant dress with the shabby appearance of the little lady.

Dr. Sangster chose that morning to come down the aisle leading to the door where the poor elderly lady and I were standing. As I saw him striding purposefully towards the vestibule, I supposed he would go the group who were obviously important. I was wrong. This distinguished preacher made straight for the little old lady. I see him now as he took her hand and then crouched down in order to make eye contact as he spoke with her. He remained in conversation for several minutes. He seemed oblivious to everyone else. Although I was only twenty years of age, I felt sure the great man was making a mistake and that I knew better. I could see the visiting dignitaries glancing at their watches and whispering to one another. Finally, they left without having spoken to the preacher. "Surely," I thought, "they were the ones who ought to have been receiving most of the attention." Looking back on that scene with the wisdom of the years I now understand. Of course Dr. Sangster had got it right. He instinctively went *to where he was needed most.*

The first call upon the church and its leaders is to go to those whose needs are the most pressing. There is no shortage of those who are eager for the photo opportunites and who can be found where the publicity or the opportunities for self advancement are the greatest. This, however, is not the Jesus way.

Luke does not tell us whether or not there were any important individuals present in the synagogue that day. The one Jesus turned to was the one who needed him most. And we honor and love him for that. Jesus did more than give good advice to that woman in the synagogue. He restored her dignity and self-worth. That is good news!

He touched her. I wonder how long it had been since she had experienced a human touch? There is a therapy in the touch that comes from genuine love and concern. And when he spoke to her we can be certain he would have looked her in the eyes; we cannot imagine Jesus who was all compassion, speaking to the top of her head! *But how would he have made eye contact?* There could be only one way. Like Dr. Sangster, he would have had to go down on one knee and stoop to her. To think that the One we call Lord and Master crouched down in order to look into the eyes of this woman. We must remember of Whom we speak. This is the One of whom Paul would write, "it pleased the Father that in Him should all fullness dwell"[2] (Col. 1:19). Jesus, the Lamb of God who takes away the sin of the world, was kneeling before a poor stooped woman! Heaven would be hushed at such an awesome spectacle.

The greatest blessing conferred on the woman with the bent back in the gospel story was not the ability to look people in the eyes. Marvelous as that was, there was conferred upon her something even more wonderful. She was affirmed to be a daughter of Abraham; a person of unique worth and significance within the plan and purpose of God. She was reminded that she was fashioned in the divine likeness and it was this awareness which enabled her to walk tall even before her bent back was cured. The restoration of the container in which her personhood was carried was a bonus.

Each of us is stooped over. No two of us are alike. The cause of our infirmity is unique to each individual. For one it is the result of an emotional trauma. For another it is the consequence of some mental distress. For yet others there are perhaps physical or spiritual factors at work. To each of us Jesus comes. He who is Lord of all stoops to our level and reaches out to touch our infirmity. He gives us the grace to walk tall and be freed from our infirmity. Wholeness begins with inner restoration and it begins now.

Note

1. J. Wallace Hamilton, "Overwhelmed" (n.p.: Spiritual Life Publishers, 1968) 31.

REGINALD MALLETT is an evangelist for the Methodist Church in England. He is a doctor of medicine and has been a practicing physician for thirty-five years. He preaches all over the world.

── 11. ──
Feeling Like a Bowling Pin

MARGARET MOERS WENIG

*U*netane tokef kedushat hayom.
Let us declare how utterly holy is this day and how terrifying . . .

B'rosh hashanah yikatevun, uv'yom tzom kippur yechatemun.
On Rosh Hashanah it is written, and on Yom Kippur it is sealed,
how many shall pass on and how many shall be created;
who shall live and who shall die;
who shall see ripe old age and who shall not;
who shall perish by fire and who by water;
who by hunger and who by thirst;
who by earthquake and who by plague;
who by strangling and who by stoning;
who shall be secure and who shall be driven;
who shall be tranquil and who shall be troubled;
who shall be poor and who shall be rich;
who shall be humbled and who shall be honored.[1]

In response to this passage, a student of mine described feeling like a bowling pin—standing in formation in a bowling lane, hearing all around her the sound of bowling balls hitting the lane, rolling down it, sometimes ending in the gutter, often crashing into pins. She described seeing the pins in front of her and beside her falling and finding herself standing nearly alone, fallen pins at her feet. She described knowing that it was only a matter of time until the ball hit her too.

The bowling pin has no control over its destiny. It is a passive recipient of whatever fate rolls its way. The pin cannot dodge the oncoming ball. It cannot decide to up and walk away and leave the dangerous fast lane. It cannot take shelter behind another object that could deflect the ball's course. And, once hit, a pin cannot lean upon another pin for support until it regains the strength to stand on its own again.

The bowling pin is an inanimate object with no control over its own life course—the bowling pin has no mind or will or ability to move. The bowling pin is nothing like us.

Then why are there times when we feel just like a bowling pin?

If you have ever spent twenty minutes wearing a disposable paper gown, sitting on a cold gray table waiting for the radiologist to walk in the door; if you have ever watched, as if from a distance, as the radiologist manipulates the machine, or your body, in order to photograph the section in question; if you have ever stared at a screen as a picture emerges of insides you didn't know you had and wondered what the dark and light shapes and shades might mean; if you have ever sat in a waiting room, dressed again in street clothes, waiting to be called in to receive the doctor's diagnosis, then you know why, even though we have a mind and a will and the capacity to exercise them, we nonetheless identify with the bowling pin.

You look around you at the other people in the waiting room and you know that they too may be ill. You think about your friends and siblings whom you have seen knocked down, then you know why we identify with the bowling pin. You know what it feels like to stand exposed, with no control, just waiting for the bowling ball to hit, maybe this time, maybe next.

People who are living with illness know, as writer Paul Cowen put it, that there are two realms in this world: the realm of the ill and the realm of the not yet ill. Unless we die suddenly, most of us will one day find ourselves sitting in the waiting room waiting for the diagnosis, wondering if the bowling ball is going to hit this time or the next.

At times like those we may be tempted to pray, "Please, God, let the test be negative. Please, God, let the tumor be benign. Please, God, don't let me be positive." Our tradition teaches that such a prayer is uttered in vain. We cannot expect the past to be altered or a present fact to be made null and void. Our tradition teaches: *If you see a fire burning in your city, you may not pray that the house not be yours. For if the fire has already started, whether or not the house is yours has already been determined.*

We should not pray that a building that is already on fire not be ours or that a tumor that has already grown not be malignant. For even before the diagnosis is revealed to us, the nature of the tumor is already established. It might as well have been "written on Rosh Hashanah and sealed on Yom Kippur." No wonder we feel like a bowling pin.

But the *Unetane tokef* doesn't end with the words "On Rosh Hashanah it is written, on Yom Kippur it is sealed." *Unetane tokef* doesn't end with the givens of life over which we have no control. *Unetane tokef* doesn't end with a curse, but continues with a promise:

U'teshuvah, utefilah, utzedakah maavirin et roa hagezera.

Turning, prayer, and righteousness temper the severity of the decree.

Teshuvah, tefilah, utzedakah do not promise to cure the illness, forestall the disability, or reverse the decline but to mitigate, sometimes slightly, sometimes substantially, the implications of the disease. If you have received a diagnosis of AIDS or cancer, heart disease or a benign tumor in a sensitive spot, then *teshuvah, tefilah, utzedakah* can temper the severity of the decree.

Teshuvah

Teshuvah means turning or turning back to God who loves you and turning or turning back to people who love you, willingly accepting their love.

Teshuvah also means repentance; examining your deeds, confessing wrongdoings, making amends, and asking for forgiveness. A man with a serious illness once insisted to me that his disease was a punishment for his sins. I argued with him vigorously, to no avail. He did not seek renewed health because he believed he deserved to be ill. To such patients, *teshuvah*, repentance, might free them from burdensome feelings of guilt to long wholeheartedly for and believe they deserve recovery.

Tefilah

Tefilah means prayer, opening our hearts and mouths and, without inhibition, expressing all the fears, the anger, the doubt, the sadness, the joy, the thanks, and the hope that come with being human and vulnerable. Prayer means saying, with the psalmist, "Out of the depths I cry to you, O LORD" (Ps. 130:1). Prayer means arguing with God as did Levi Yitzhak of Berdichev.[2] Prayer means singing, "O Lord, hold my hand while I run this race." Prayer means pleading in the evening time, *"Hashkiveinu Adonai Eloheinu, leshalom; vehaamideynu malkeinu l'chayim. O God, may I lie down to sleep in peace and awaken the next morning to renewed life."* Prayer means thanking God each morning when we wake, *"Modah ani lifanecha, melech chay vekayam, shehecheҳarti bi nishmati be chemla rabah emunatecha.* I thank you God for restoring my life to me." And once we are finally able to get out of bed and into the bathroom, even if it is with much pain or with a companion's assistance, prayer means saying, "Blessed are you, O God, who has created our bodies with wisdom—combining veins, arteries, and vital organs into a finely balanced network." Prayer means whispering, as we are wheeled into the operating room, *"Beyado afkid ruchi, b'eyt ishan v'airah, v'im ruchi geviyati adonai li v'lo ira.* Into your hands I entrust my spirit as I sleep, and when I awaken, and with my spirit my body also—you are with me, I shall not fear." And then, when we awake in the recovery room, prayer means reciting *"Shehecheyyanu.* Thank you, God, for enabling me to make it to this moment."

Prayer means not holding back, not trying to hide the tears or the fear, the loneliness or the yearning. Prayer means noticing the love that surrounds us rather than taking it for granted. It means expressing gratitude for the mental and physical capabilities we still have even if some have been lost to us.

Tzedakah

Tzedakah means doing righteousness, remembering that in the Jewish cosmology, human beings were created for a purpose: to restore a measure of wholeness to the world through righteousness and love. *Tzedakah* means having a reason to wake up in the morning, knowing that you are needed. There is a neighbor, even sicker than you are, who needs a friendly phone call. There is a grandchild who needs your love.

I think about a member of this congregation who has survived two major heart operations, the collapse of one lung, surgery on her hip, shoulder, and eyes, who can barely see the notes on the page, and can barely move her fingers. Yet she still teaches poor children to play the piano. I believe that her mission helps keep her alive. *Tzedakah* is a mission that keeps a human being from being bored to death.

We are not bowling pins, merely passive victims of whatever comes rolling our way. We have a measure of control over our ability to fight against or to live with illness. For one thing, we Jews value the power of the physician as illustrated in this midrash:

> Rabbis Ishmael and Akiva were walking in the streets of Jerusalem along with a companion. They met a sick person who asked them, "Masters, how can I be healed?" The rabbis advised him to take a certain medicine till he felt better.
>
> The rabbis' companion challenged them, "Who created this sick man?" "The Holy One," replied the rabbis. Their companion continued his argument, "The Holy One created him, but you think you can heal him? Why do you presume to interfere in an area that is not yours?"
>
> The rabbis, pointing to the sickle their companion was carrying, retorted, "What is your occupation?" "Farming," the companion answered. "Who created the earth?" the rabbis asked him. "The Holy One," answered the companion. The rabbis continued, "The Holy One created the earth, but you

think you can plant and harvest it? How can you presume to interfere in an area that is not yours?"

The companion answered, "You know as well as I, if I do not plow and plant and fertilize the field, nothing will grow in it." "True," said the rabbis. "Just as the crops do not grow unless a farmer sows and fertilizes, so too the body cannot heal without medicine—its fertilizer and the doctor—its farmer."

We surely value the physician's role. And yet we have always acknowledged the role of less tangible factors in the process of surviving and sometimes even healing.

Eight hundred years ago, Maimonides, the great Jewish physician and philosopher, observed the salutary effects on a patient of such things as music, hope, laughter, and a relationship with a caregiver.

Can we explain in physiological terms the connection that Maimonides observed between a patient's spiritual well-being and her physical well-being? Surgeon Bernie Siegel described it this way:

> Every tissue and organ in the body is controlled by complex interaction among hormones secreted by our endocrine glands and circulated through the bloodstream. This mixture is controlled by the master gland, the pituitary, which is, in turn, controlled by chemical secretions and nerve impulses from the neighboring hypothalamus. This tiny region of the brain regulates most of the body's unconscious maintenance processes such as heartbeat, breathing, blood pressure, temperature, and so forth.
>
> Nerve fibers enter the hypothalamus from nearly all other regions of the brain so that intellectual and emotional processes occurring elsewhere in the brain affect the body.
>
> For example, . . . child development researchers discovered psychosocial dwarfism—a . . . syndrome in which . . . the brain's emotional center or limbic system [in a child growing up in a hostile environment] acts upon the nearby hypothalamus to shut off the pituitary gland's production of growth hormone.
>
> The immune system consists of more than a dozen different types of white blood cells concentrated in the spleen, thymus gland, and lymph nodes, patrolling the entire body through

the blood and lymphatic systems. . . . Research has shown heretofore unknown nerves connecting the thymus and spleen directly to the hypothalamus. Other work has proven that white blood cells respond directly to some of the same chemicals that carry messages from one nerve cell to another. . . .[3]

Thus, like the unconscious body maintenance processes, the immune system too is controlled by the brain and affected by thoughts and emotions.

Siegel cited research that suggests the healing power of hearty laughter. Laughter "produces complete, relaxed action of the diaphragm, exercising the lungs, increasing the blood's oxygen level, and gently toning the entire cardiovascular system." According to some, "laughter also increases the production of a class of brain chemicals called catecholamines," which can activate a part of the immune system that reduces inflammation and increases the production of endorphins, the body's natural opiates.[4]

Siegel cited a study at the Menninger Foundation in Topeka, Kansas, in which people who were in love were found to have reduced levels of lactic acid in their blood, making them less tired, as well as higher levels of endorphins, making them euphoric and less subject to pain. Their white blood cells also responded better when faced with infections, and, thus, they got fewer colds.

Some suggest that unresolved grief depresses immunity. Some suggest that a patient is less likely to suffer side effects of radiation treatment if he imagines golden beams of sunshine entering his body rather than killer rays. Some suggest that touching—stroking, hugging, kissing—is essential to physical growth and mental development of infants. Some, such as Dr. Siegel, have come to believe that the resolution of conflicts, the realization of authentic self (with purpose), spiritual awareness, and love release energy that enhances the chemistry of healing. Even if these particular studies prove scientifically inadequate, our sense of the connection between mind and body remains strong enough to propel further research.[5]

Is a failure to recover due to a patient's failure to muster the spiritual resources to promote healing? Far be it from any of us to pass such a judgment! Any individual case of illness and recovery or illness and further decline is a function of so many different factors, far be it from any of us to presume to know whether or not it was in the patient's power to overcome genetic or environmental factors or even to mitigate their impact. No, laughter, love, and visions of golden beams of sunshine do not deny the reality of the virus or the tumor. Laughter, love, and visions of golden beams of sunshine do not deny the reality of genetic or environmental factors over which we, and even our doctors, may have little control. No, laughter, love, and visions of golden beams of sunshine do not deny the fact that, for reasons beyond our control, we most likely will become ill. "*Be rosh hashanah yikatevun uvayom tzom kippur yichatemun.* On Rosh Hashanah it is written, and on Yom Kippur it is sealed," as if we had no more control than inanimate bowling pins.

These, however, are not *Unetane tokef*'s last words. For us, the diagnosis is not always the first word, and the prognosis is not always the last word. "Never underestimate the capacity of the human mind and body to survive and sometimes even to regenerate even when the prospects seem most wretched."[6]

No denying it. The bowling ball is there and it is real and it is coming our way, but we are not entirely powerless in the face of it. For we believe, we hope, we pray that *teshuvah, tefilah, utzedakah* can temper the severity of the decree.

(*I turned and looked directly at Harriet Appel, who had just been diagnosed with a brain tumor.*)

Dear Harriet, tomorrow you will enter the hospital so that on Tuesday the surgeon can remove a tumor from your brain. We know that you are frightened. We know that as you lie in bed on Monday night wondering what the next day will bring, you will feel very much alone. But please know that though it will be you alone who will be wheeled into surgery on Tuesday, in every other sense you are not alone. We will be thinking about you, we will be praying for you. As soon as visitors are permitted, we will come to sit beside you.

I know you feel completely at the mercy of your doctors who made the diagnosis, recommended the surgery, and scheduled the surgery for Yom Kippur over your objection. They will perform the surgery, but you are not completely powerless. Turn to those who love you, express your feelings in prayer, know that you have a reason to recover: to live to see your grandchildren married and to help us usher this congregation, to which you helped give birth, into the next generation.

(At this point, I stepped down from the pulpit. I walked up to Harriet, who was sitting on the aisle, and held her hands. The congregation spontaneously stood up. Together we prayed.)

> May God who blessed our ancestors, Abraham, Isaac and Jacob, Sarah, Rebecca, Rachel and Leah, grant blessed healing to you, Harriet Appel. May God be with you in your illness and give you patience, hope, and courage. And may God so endow your attending physicians and nurses with insight and skill that, by their efforts, and if possible, by yours as well, you be restored to health and vigor of body and mind.
>
> Rabbi: *Ana el na fefa na la. Beharot la noam zivecha. Az titcha-zek, v'tit rapey. V'hayta la simchat olam.*
>
> Congregation: Please God, help heal her. Show her the light of your face. May she be strengthened and may joy be hers.
>
> Rabbi: *Yivarechecha Adonai v'yishmerecha.*
> Congregation: May God bless you and protect you.
> Rabbi: *Yaer Adonai panav elecha vichunecha.*
> Congregation: May God's face shine mercy upon you.
> Rabbi: *Yisa Adonai panav elecha v'yasem lecha shalom.*
> Congregation: May God look lovingly upon you and grant you peace of mind.

Notes

1. "*Unetane tokef*" is a medieval liturgical poem, prominent in our prayers on Rosh Hashanah and on Yom Kippur. The year I gave this sermon, Harriet

Appel, a founding member of our congregation, already in her eighties, had just been diagnosed with a brain tumor, which, though benign, had to be removed. When the surgeon scheduled her operation for Yom Kippur and refused to reschedule it, Harriet and all of us were "spooked." Surgery on Yom Kippur felt like a bad omen. On Rosh Hashanah (the occasion of this sermon), ten days before the surgery and a day before her pre-operative admission to the hospital, Harriet's well-being was foremost in our minds. Harriet had been widowed years earlier, many of her peers had died, and despite her attentive, if small, family, her regular presence at worship, and her role as an outspoken trustee of the congregation, Harriet felt lonely. Her acerbic tongue made it difficult for newer, younger members of the congregation to grow close to her. Nonetheless, we cherished her and considered her a vital member of our community. The goal of this sermon was to try to take the edge off of the fear Harriet felt and we all shared and, most of all, to show Harriet that the congregation loved her. A few years later, in the only compliment Harriet ever paid me, she attributed her survival and recovery from surgery to the prayers we offered her at the close of this sermon.

2. An early chassidic master born in Galica in 1740. See Anson Laytner, *Arguing with God* (Northvale, N.J.: Jason Aronson Press, 1990).

3. Bernie S. Siegel, *Love, Medicine & Miracles* (New York: Harper & Row, 1986), pp. 67-68.

4. Ibid., p. 144.

5. In the twenty years since this sermon was given, the field of Integrative Medicine has mushroomed. Note, for example, the work by Jon Kabat-Zinn, PhD, at the Stress Reduction and Relaxation Program at the University of Massachusetts Medical Center. For a description, see Nancy Waring, "Mindfulness Meditation: Studies Show That Awareness Practices Promote Healing," *Hippocrates*, from the publishers of the *New England Journal of Medicine* 14, no. 7 (July 2000).

6. Norman Cousins, *Anatomy of an Illness as Perceived by the Patient* (New York: Norton, 1979), p. 48.

MARGARET MOERS WENIG is Rabbi Emerita of Beth Am, The People's Temple, and instructor in Liturgy and Homiletics at Hebrew Union College-Jewish Institute of Religion, in New York.

—— 12. ——
When the Phone Rings

1 Kings 17:17-24; Luke 7:11-17

DAVID T. TAYLOR

Hello, David, this is Dan, we need your help. We need to have a funeral for our daughter Sarah. She died last night." Sarah Jeanne was twenty-three months old, and she died in her father's arms.

"David," Andrea, our church secretary said, "that call was from Mark. MaryLu has died." MaryLu was fifty-one, the church moderator and former senior deacon. Her two-year struggle with cancer was now over.

The voice mail message was retrieved that Saturday morning, in the midst of the church's festive Holiday Fair and Cookie Walk. "Hello, this is Donna, my son, Eric, was one of the three boys killed last night in the accident." Three teenage boys and a father of two children perished in a fiery automobile crash just as the Advent season of hope, peace, joy, and love was in its first week.

When the phone rings, wouldn't it be nice if you, or I, or the church possessed the healing power of Elijah?

"Give me your son," Elijah said to the grieving widow, whose son's illness was so severe that there was no breath left in him. Elijah then implored God, "O LORD my God, let this child's life come into him again" (1 Kgs. 17:21).

But why couldn't Sarah Jeanne's life come into her again?

When the phone rings, wouldn't it be nice if we possessed Elijah's resurrection authority?

Elijah picked up the child, brought him down from the upstairs chamber, and gave him to his mother. Then Elijah said, "See, your son is alive" (1 Kgs. 17:23).

But, my Lord and my God, why couldn't someone pick up seventeen-year-old Eric and give him over to his mother saying, "See, your son is alive"?

When the phone rings, wouldn't it be nice if we were somehow able to say to someone like Mark, as Jesus said to the widow in Nain, "Do not weep. . . . God has looked favorably upon his people" (Luke 7:13, 16).

When the phone rings, what can we say to someone who has lost a baby girl?

What can we say to someone who has lost a teenage son?

What can we say to someone who has lost a beloved wife?

What can we say? What can the church say? What can the pastor say? What can the faith possibly say at times such as these?

What healing power is available to the church at these moments of death and finality?

When there is no prophet Elijah, no miracle-working Jesus, no apparent power or authority to raise the dead to new life, what is left?

At times such as these, what ministry of healing remains for the church?

The phone also rang for me one summer when I was in seminary, working with an urban church's ministry of fellowship and outreach to members and nonmembers alike. It was a Friday afternoon, and I was preparing the van to take a group of young adults to a summer concert featuring Linda Rondstadt and James Taylor.

The church secretary said the call was for me, from the pastor of my home church, "David, your father had a heart attack playing tennis, and he is now unconscious."

I drove the one hour home. In the emergency room at the hospital, he went into cardiac arrest, but they were able to bring life back into him. Nine weeks later, however, Dad died, never regaining consciousness.

What was the church's ministry to me in those nine weeks? My remembrance of the church's healing love and power are as vivid in my mind as if they had happened right after this morning's first cup of coffee.

At the church where I was working, lay and clergy dropped everything to take over my duties. Over those many weeks of our family's vigil at my father's bedside, their telephone calls of compassion and concern seemed to find me wherever I was. Their prayers in worship touched my heart. Their presence at the memorial service will never be forgotten. And a friend of the family, an Episcopal priest who a few years later became a bishop, stopped by with these comforting and consoling words, "Give thanks for his life. Continue your conversations with him. If you keep his memory alive, he will live."

In the loss and tragedy of death that I was experiencing, the church had a powerful word of healing to be spoken. Just as the woman said to Elijah, "The word of the LORD in your mouth is truth" (1 Kgs. 17:24), the church had a word of truth to speak to me.

When the phone rings, the church has a word to speak. It has a truth to tell. It has the good news of Jesus Christ to proclaim. A great prophet has risen among us! God has looked favorably upon us. When the phone rings, the church has a Word to tell and a love to share.

But can that Word be spoken—and can that Word be heard—at those sad times for families who have lost loved ones?

The funeral service for little Sarah was a celebration of love and a celebration of life. As we sat and listened to her favorite music, from *The Lion King*, we were reminded of the "circle of life" of which we all are privileged, for a while, to be a part.

Two years later, when family, friends, and the community gathered to dedicate a playground in Sarah's memory, I offered the following words in prayer:

> We now dedicate this playground as a place to share life. We rejoice and we give thanks for the unbounded, joyous experience of life that will happen here. We give thanks for playing, jumping, and climbing. We give thanks for skipping, swinging, and sliding. We give thanks for riding, running, and bouncing.

We give thanks for the laughter and the giggles, the gleeful and happy sounds of children, the conversation and new friendships between parents, and for the simple enjoyment of this playground—this playground of love, this playground of life.

Gracious God, we do give you thanks for your precious gifts of life and love. And we give you thanks that Sarah's life and love are very much alive and will remain forever with us in your unbroken circle of life.

MaryLu will be remembered forever at the church she loved, and at the high school where she taught, coached, and earned the respect of teachers, students, and parents. What then is the Word to share, the good news to proclaim, and God's favor to be celebrated amidst this devastating loss to so many different communities?

To the congregation in the New England meetinghouse and to the overflow crowd in the church's social hall, I shared my experience with Mark and MaryLu in the week before her death. During that visit to their home that they had built together, we shared in a time of prayer, scripture reading, and the sacrament of Holy Communion.

After reading a psalm or two that I had chosen, they asked me to read Psalm 19, a psalm that had offered them great strength, great comfort, and great hope.

And so, as we gathered close around MaryLu's bedside, I read these words from her Bible,

> The law of the LORD is perfect,
>   reviving the soul;
> the decrees of the LORD are sure,
>   making wise the simple;
> the precepts of the LORD are right,
>   rejoicing the heart;
> the commandment of the LORD is clear,
>   enlightening the eyes;
> the fear of the LORD is pure,
>   enduring forever;

the ordinances of the LORD are true
 and righteous altogether. . . .
Let the words of my mouth and the meditation of my heart
 be acceptable to you,
O LORD, my rock and my redeemer. (Ps. 19:7-9, 14)

God—Creator, Christ, and Holy Spirit—was the Word for MaryLu's life. It was the truth for her life. It was God's favor for her life. It was the good news that the church proclaimed to her and to her family. It was the good news that they proclaimed to us. And it was the good news that sustained her, and them, even in the midst of the sadness and tragedy of her death. But what about the tragedy of death, during the Advent and Christmas season, of three high-school seniors and a father of two young children? The Friday-night collision of two cars in a blazing inferno left the families, the high school, and the entire community with many unanswered questions.

What can the faith possibly say at times such as these?

What healing power is left to the church at these moments of death and finality?

When there is no prophet Elijah, no miracle-working Jesus, no apparent power or authority to raise the dead to life from the wreckage on the streets, what then *is* left?

When the phone rings, what word of hope and love can be spoken? What is the church's healing ministry at times such as these?

Another New England meetinghouse is filled to capacity and overflowing into adjacent rooms. The sea of three hundred youthful, high-school faces dominates the congregation. This would be the first of three funeral services for them on this cold December day. Area television cameras would capture their somber march down Main Street to attend the other two services.

Printed on the bulletin cover for Eric's funeral service was a single candle and the scripture verse that Eric had chosen to read the year before at the ceremony of candle lighting and the reaffirmation of his baptismal vows prior to being confirmed:

Jesus spoke . . . , "I am the light of the world. Whoever follows me will never walk in darkness." (John 8:12)

That morning we gave thanks to God for Eric's seventeen wonderful years. We gave thanks to God for the incredible gift of Eric's life. And we gave thanks to God for the awesome gift of the life of Jesus Christ, whose light has made it so we will never walk in darkness, ever again.

When the phone rings, and when it seems as if the darkness has overcome all the life in the world, the church has a Life to share.

When the phone rings, and when it seems as if the darkness has overcome all the light in the world, the church has a Light to share.

When the phone rings, and when it seems as if the darkness has overcome all the love in the world, the church has a Love to share.

The church must be ready, when the phone rings.

DAVID T. TAYLOR is the pastor at First Church of Christ, Congregational (UCC) in Glastonbury, Connecticut. He is on the board of directors of Back Bay Mission, Biloxi, Mississippi, and is a member of the United Church of Christ Toward the 21st Century Planning Committee.

13.
Healing the Infirmity of Spirit

(Luke 13:10-11)
BARBARA LUNDBLAD

She had grown accustomed to looking at feet. After eighteen years bent down, she knew people by their bunions! Who knows what the diagnosis was? Osteoporosis, perhaps, or years of women's work—lifting, scrubbing, cleaning, washing feet. The text only tells us she had an ailment that crippled her. According to the RSV, she had "a spirit of infirmity" (v. 11). Isn't it likely that she also had an "infirmity of spirit"? Oh, this was not her own doing. She could have coped with her physical condition; indeed, she had learned to live with it for eighteen years. But it was the way she was treated by others that caused this other infirmity, often more devastating than the first. It was the way people sometimes spoke over her back as though she weren't even there. Or walked away from her in the middle of a sentence, or kept their distance as though her condition could be contagious. It took more than a little gumption to come to Sabbath worship because she knew some considered her condition to be God's punishment for some sin—either hers or her parents.

Nancy Mairs knows something about such things. Nancy, a gifted writer, has lived for years with multiple sclerosis that gets worse year by year. Her book, *Waist-high in the World*, describes her vantage point from a wheelchair. "The truth is," she says, "that unless you are squatting or six years old, I can never look you straight in the eye."[1] That's not so different from looking only at feet. Mairs gives voice to what it means to have an "infirmity of spirit."

The fact that the soundness of the body so often serves as a metaphor for its moral health, its deterioration thus implying moral degeneracy, puts me and my kind in a quandary. How can I possibly be "good"? Let's face it, wicked witches are not just ugly (as sin); they're also bent and misshapen (crooked). I am bent and misshapen, therefore, ugly, therefore wicked. And I have no way to atone.[2]

Don't we say things like "keep your chin up," "stand tall," "walk on your own two feet," and "look me straight in the eye"? Nobody wants to "take it lying down." And who wants to be left "without a leg to stand on"?

It's not hard to imagine that, after eighteen years bent down, the woman had an infirmity of spirit. Did anyone bend down to look into her eyes? Did anyone think to say, "Can I get you anything from the market?" or "Would you like to walk to synagogue with me?" Did anyone ever touch her?

The text doesn't tell us such things. We only know that she appeared in the synagogue as Jesus was teaching. She doesn't go to him or cry out for attention. Indeed, she might have gone unnoticed—except, when Jesus saw her come in, he called her over. Was he in the middle of a sentence when she entered? No matter. She became more important than what he was teaching. Listen carefully to what happened next. Jesus said to her, "Woman, you are freed from your infirmity" (v. 12 RSV). After saying this, Jesus laid his hands on her, and she stood up straight and began praising God. But his first words are very important: "Woman, you are set free from your infirmity." Even before she stood up straight, even before her physical condition changed, even before she was cured, she was *healed*.

She was set free. Was that what was so upsetting to the religious leaders? Did this act of healing undermine the good order of the Sabbath day? Note that the leaders didn't chastise Jesus; they shouted at the crowds, including the woman who was now praising God. I wonder what she was thinking? After all those years looking at feet, she stood up to see faces contorted with rage. Why, it was enough to make her look down again! While she was praising God, the religious leaders were scolding the crowd.

Of course, Jesus was still there, and heard their outburst. He returned to his teaching, but now the subject had changed. He took upon himself the charges hurled at the woman and the crowd, and began to argue case law like a rabbi: "Does not each of you on the sabbath untie his ox or his ass from the manger, and lead it away to water it? And ought not this woman, a daughter of Abraham whom Satan bound for eighteen years, be loosed from this bond on the sabbath day?" (Luke 13:15-16 RSV). I wonder what she was thinking about while Jesus was talking. Maybe she thought about the tenth commandment: "Neither shall you covet your neighbor's wife; and you shall not desire your neighbor's house, his field, or his manservant, or his maidservant, his ox, or his ass, or anything that is your neighbor's" (Deut. 5:21 RSV). When I was in confirmation class years ago, we tried to say the words really fast. And when you say the words fast, *wife* and *ox* and *ass* blur together, as though they were all about the same, all a man's property. I have no idea if she thought about such things when Jesus talked about untying an ox or a donkey on the Sabbath day, but she must have been delighted when Jesus called her a "daughter of Abraham." Part of the chosen people, a member of the family cherished by God.

This was no small thing—for the bent-over woman must have felt judged because of her condition and shunned by others even within her own family. She had learned to live a life alone. Kathy Black is a teacher of worship and preaching; she is also a person who lives with a chronic illness that can paralyze her without warning. In her book, *A Healing Homiletic,* she says, "It would be nice not to have to live with the limitations posed by the physical disability, but it is the social isolation and alienation people experience that is the most difficult."[3] That's why curb cuts in the sidewalk and kneeling buses are so important. That's why people—even people in a hurry—sit patiently in New York City while the driver gets up, goes to the back, lowers the lift and raises it again to bring a person in a wheelchair or electric cart onto the bus. It's a lot of trouble, some say, and very expensive.

After the terrible attack against the World Trade Center, people with disabilities have been haunted in particular ways. Some, no doubt, read the story of a man named Abe who could have walked downstairs to safety, but stayed with his friend who was paraplegic. Both of them perished when the towers fell. Some people with disabilities now wonder if certain jobs will be closed to them, if they'll be limited to jobs on the ground floor. How can we be communities of healing where those with disabilities gather with the temporarily able-bodied (that is, people like me)? Where we pray for one another, yet understand that healing may come even when a cure is not in sight? How can we listen to the voices of those who live with disabilities so they can become our teachers? How can we follow Jesus' example and help set people free from their infirmities of spirit?

"I mean to make a map," says Nancy Mairs. She's talking about a map to negotiate the unknown territory ahead of her, a map to help her through what is now foreign terrain, a map that might help others who will someday feel their bodies giving way. "My infinitely harder task," she says, "is to conceptualize not merely a habitable body but a habitable world: a world that wants me in it."[4]

On this St. Luke's Day, many will come forward for the laying on of hands and prayers of healing. We pray for ourselves and for one another. We pray also for a habitable world, a world that wants Nancy Mairs and other people with disabilities in it. We pray God's healing hand upon our beloved city and all its people: those fighting against great odds to recover, those struggling with fear, those longing for security that will never be what it once was. We pray for all who live not only with a spirit of infirmity but also with an infirmity of spirit that bends them low.

Come, O Jesus, come to this day and touch us with your grace. Set free all that binds us and call us once again to be a community of healing in this broken world. Amen.

Notes

1. Nancy Mairs, *Waist-High in the World: A Life among the Nondisabled* (Boston: Beacon Press, 1996), 6.

2. Ibid., 57.
3. Kathy Black, A *Healing Homiletic: Preaching and Disability* (Nashville: Abingdon Press, 1996), 183.
4. Mairs, *Waist-High in the World*, 65.

BARBARA LUNDBLAD was pastor at Our Saviour's Atonement Lutheran Church in Manhattan for seventeen years. In 1997 she joined the faculty of Union Theological Seminary as associate professor of preaching. She has taught preaching at Yale Divinity School, Princeton Theological Seminary, Hebrew Union College, and the Doctor of Ministry program in preaching at the Association of Chicago Theological Schools. She is author of *Transforming the Stone: Preaching through Resistance to Change*.

— 14. —
Healing through Via Negativa

Mark 5:25-34

E. Lee Hancock

Last year I was in a New York City parking garage waiting to retrieve my car for what seemed to be an interminable period of time. A swelling crowd was shrinking the garage and filling the air with electricity. Having parked in the vicinity of the United Nations, I thought the crowd signaled the presence of a dignitary, head of state, or the president! When a white SUV shot out of the bowels of the garage, young fans swarmed the car, screaming, pressing in, slowing the car and trying to get in. For one moment I glimpsed the world-famous rock star, wanly waving to his fans, surrounded by bodyguards, as the driver desperately inched his way out of the garage in a mad dash to get away without rendering bodily harm. I was shocked by the sight. Whether out of curiosity or devotion or some misguided hope of a brush with the divine, the crowd was pushing, shoving, screaming, wanting to see him, to be close to him, to touch him—and so it was with the crowds around Jesus.

In his time, Jesus, too, was an object of controversy, curiosity, suspicion, and hope. Word was spreading about this charismatic prophet, this man who thumbed his nose at the religious authorities and called attention to the suffering and the poor, the shunned and the misfit. His "in your face" attitude drew fire from the religious leaders for his confrontational ways that flagrantly defied the rules that ordered common life. And to make matters worse, it was the riffraff, the poor, the down and out, the dirty, the desperate, and the needy who followed him, pursued him for a look, a glimpse, a touch. His healing power was unmistakable. The stories of his ability to do magic—to order the sea to quiet, turn water into wine, feed five thousand—were enough to draw the attention of the desperate, hopeless, and needy. No one, not even his own disciples, knew what to make of this prophet. Charlatan? Quack? Healer? Messiah? His healing power attracted rich and poor alike. Their need was the great leveler. Whether powerful or humble, out of desperation or hope, people were drawn to Jesus for healing.

The fifth chapter of Mark gathers together several healing narratives. After healing the Gerasene demoniac—accompanied by his bodyguards, the disciples—Jesus is begged by the powerful Jairus, a leader of the synagogue, to rescue his beloved daughter from the jaws of death. Entranced by his power and possibility, the curious, the captivated, the naysayer, and the devotee alike swarmed alongside of Jesus, tracking his moves, dogging his steps. The biblical narrative is interrupted with a story about the needs of an unnamed woman. Jesus' trip to Jairus's house is diverted by his encounter with a woman who had been hemorrhaging for twelve years. Her bleeding rendered her ritually unclean, cut off from society. A bleeding woman could not leave her house, could not be in physical contact with any man, and surely could not be among a crowd lest she brush against a man and make him unclean. For twelve long years she had been isolated, cut off from society by her condition, dying a social death of isolation and alienation. Doctors had failed her, an experience of despair and hopelessness known to many of us. But this day, encouraged by the rumors about Jesus and armed by desperation, she jumped into the crowd, bumping, swimming, moving toward the one who might restore her life— heal the wound of her body that cut her off from the community, from the very life she longed to have. Gaining speed and proximity, in one long gesture she reached out to touch him. As her fingers brushed his cloak, the text tells us that Jesus felt the power go out of him. How did he know? Was she grasping for the divine energy coursing through his body? He turned to his disciples and asked, "Who touched my garments?" (v. 30 RSV).

Most likely annoyed, the disciples replied, "You see the crowd pressing around you, and yet you say 'Who touched me?'" (v. 31 RSV). Undeterred, Jesus turned around, searching the crowd for the one who touched him. The terrified woman, the one who knew about the transaction of power and life, when she realized that her bleeding had stopped, confessed to Jesus what she had done.

In that swift moment, what did she know, and what had she done? Was she grasping for the divine energy coursing through his body? How did she know he possessed what she needed? Drawn to his power, driven by her desperation, she reached out across the social chasm that cut her off and condemned her to death, to touch hope. And she was healed—healed from her physical affliction, saved from her social isolation and ritual impurity, restored to wholeness. Her faith in the possibility of healing made her well, literally saved her, for the Greek word used for healing in this passage is *sodzo*, a term for healing that implies salvation. She was restored to wholeness in her physical body, just as she was reintroduced, re-membered into the corporate body. This unknown woman was not simply cured; she was saved from social as well as physical death she suffered daily that cut her off from her community. She had faced a death sentence as debilitating as the slow bleeding she endured.

In our time, for over two decades, people with HIV/AIDS have been dying agonizing social deaths as virulent as the virus itself. This unnamed woman in Mark teaches us that healing is not only a matter of being corporally cured, it is a matter of being restored to membership in the body politic.

She also reminds us of the spiritual truth of desperation and vulnerability. They are often the means to a spiritual path that can lead to healing, blessing, and transformation. They can orient us to our need for healing. This spiritual path was termed by the Rhineland mystics the *via negativa*, the way of the negative.[1] It is the spiritual path through loss, through a seeming absence of God, through suffering and pain. It is the way of the desperate and the vulnerable. It is the way of our times.

We often hear the old phrase "desperate people do desperate things," taking risks fueled by vulnerability and need. Our desperation is often our way to the divine. That is the *via negativa*.

When I was twenty-four, I was crippled from a chronic disease, rheumatoid arthritis. Like the woman in Mark, I had received long treatments with many doctors, but I remained unable to walk. One evening, late at night, isolated and cut off by fatigue and immobility from a family gathering, I turned on the TV set in my in-laws' bedroom where I was resting. Flipping channels, I was drawn to a tent revival conducted by Oral Roberts, a healer whom I regarded with contempt and disdain. I couldn't take my eyes off the channel. When his certainty met my desperation, I found myself accepting his invitation to lay my hands on the television set if I wanted to be healed. No instant miracles happened, but in my vulnerability and desperation, my hope was galvanized to take a risk to reach for my heart's desire: healing.

God works through the *via negativa*—the way of pain and suffering, of vulnerability and desperation. It is often a spiritual path we neither choose nor want to travel upon. It is also a journey we can find ourselves embarking upon whether we like it or not. The stories of Jarius's daughter and the woman with the issues of blood stand like bookends reminding us that anyone, regardless of status, can be called into the *via negativa*. Our choice is whether we can embrace the journey as a way to God, as a path to healing, rather than denying, rejecting, or judging the path or ourselves. It is the path to God when we feel the most cut off from body, left out of the human race. The path calls us to let go of our ideas of what makes us acceptable in the eyes of God, of what behaviors or protocols are proper or appropriate. The *via negativa* demands that we let go of all that we know and all that we expect. Desperation and vulnerability are difficult to endure, but they just might be our way to the divine. When we let them in, they might give us enough fuel to reach out in hope to the promise of healing that transcends the limits of science and human understanding and demand the divine energy that can make us whole. Thanks be to God for the unnamed woman who shows us a way to the Holy One who can make us whole. Amen.

Note

1. For a full discussion of the *via negativa*, see Matthew Fox, *Original Blessing* (Santa Fe, N. Mex.: Bear, 1983), 132-78.

E. LEE HANCOCK is the dean of Auburn Theological Seminary in New York City. She is a Presbyterian minister with special interest in healing and health care.

—— 15. ——
The Mundane Revolution

Matthew 2:13-15

GARY GUNDERSON

This is an awkward Sunday on which to preach, surprisingly so, since this is a season so drenched in meaning. The problem is that the biblical story that has carried us toward and through Christmas takes a violent, jarring, and inexplicable turn at the very moment the herald angels finish harking. We don't expect it and we don't like it.

In the traditional American rhythm of the season, we move smoothly from Advent to Christmas. Then we have a gentle, laid-back week, some of us in the office, some not, both groups accomplishing the same amount of useful work. Then we gear up for New Year's Day, an event of celebration—or at least entertainment—for most, and, for many, serious reflection about their lives. We are encouraged to think about what we did and didn't do in the previous year and especially to think of the several strategic things that would provide the breakthrough to new levels of accomplishment or happiness or accumulation or other self-improvement. The first step toward civilization begins with such hypocrisy, so that is not so bad. New Year's Day is pleasantly hypocritical. This fits us goal-oriented Americans, and I confess I like it.

But the Bible story does not reflect a time of reflection at all. It does not echo our penchant for planning and accomplishment. So we skip over it and leave it behind. But look at it again.

Jesus' mom and dad, barely recovered from the birth, have a horrible dream. They made their first act of voluntary parenting a hurried, desperate run for their lives, and, more exactly, the life of Jesus. Before Jesus could focus his eyes, he was on the run, dashing through nighttime streets soon washed with the innocent blood of thousands of infants suspected of his "crime": being the Chosen One, God's anointed, the Prince.

Herod, the petty king of the region, acted like petty warlords have done through all time. The shepherds in the fields may be dated, but Herod is as modern as a personal computer. He would know what to do in Serbia, Liberia, Somalia, Mozambique, Iraq, and a hundred other places in our tortured time. He tried to kill everyone he feared, beginning with the weakest.

Jesus' parents chose life for their baby. They fled all they knew and had hoped for and went to Africa. Across Gaza, where refugee camps still stand today, across the desert to Egypt, the place Moses left long before. To imagine their New Year's Day, look toward the hundreds of refugee enclaves today where parents huddle, trying to protect the chance for their children to survive the day, the week, the month, never mind the year.

We know nothing of Jesus' African experience—where he lived, how his parents earned money, how long he stayed. What an amazing gap! We know nothing of Jesus' most formative years—Jesus the infant, the toddler. We can only infer how Mary and Joseph kept faith with their instinctive choice for life that denied Herod's choice of death.

It is fair to look at the mature Jesus and infer the efforts his parents made to protect him and love him. In the stories we have of the mature Jesus, we are amazed to see the comfort with which he moved amid insecurity and diversity during his itinerant ministry. Where did he learn to believe in love so strongly? Clearly, unless Jesus had virgin parenting to go along with his virgin birth, Mary and Joseph performed the first miracle of his life. Long before he turned water into wine, they loved him in such a way that he could recognize, receive, and reflect God's openhanded love. Even in a first-century refugee camp, Jesus learned to look for and expect God amid human life, not just in the distant afterlife. Think how differently he could have emerged. Look only as far as the refugee camps today where the next generation of vengeance is weaned in bitterness and anger. Jesus would have been dead to us just as surely as if Herod had gotten him on the first night of his life.

No wonder we have such difficulty following the story. How do we relate to the refugee king, the peaceful prince so comfortable in the very things we fear: rootlessness, poverty, controversy?

Let me suggest that Jesus' Egyptian flight does have some lessons for us as we sit here in America, anticipating a new year. It is not the lesson that we might expect. I think we can look toward the unsung work of Jesus' parents as an example of following through on the defining choice of their lives. They chose to flee all they knew in order to give Jesus a chance; to give God's Hope a little time. It was all they could do, and they did it. Far more important, they followed through by raising him so that love had a chance to break forth through him unto all times, even unto ours.

We also make choices that demand years of incremental commitment to mature. Few of us are forced to flee or break with our past in such a violent way. But we make other choices that define us, that define the future we hope for. But we tend to focus far too heavily on the dramatic, pregnant moment of choice, the missionary's decision or the protester's moment of voluntary arrest. We elevate the event of choice, the revolutionary moment when the new commitment overcomes the inertia of past commitments. Choosing is near to the center of what defines us as a people. We like choice, we like choosing, we like to applaud others when they choose.

But Mary and Joseph quietly hint that the choosing is the easy part, even if it is sometimes the key to having any part at all. The kingdom must not only be chosen but it must also be built. The revolution may be chosen in the event of deciding, but it is only built in the daily increments of commitment that follow through.

There have been amazing changes for good in the world recently. But the things that we know should be so easy have turned out to be so very hard. We still find it out of reach to bring a clean well to every village. We haven't gotten the most rudimentary gift of modern medicine—immunization—to children who live literally within a few miles of the most modern medical equipment in history. We don't know the answer to curing AIDS, but we certainly do know about smoking, heart disease, alcohol, measles, TB, polio, and a hundred other scourges affecting millions of lives. Solving these problems should be like rolling off a log.

Any number of international conferences with presidents and potentates have delineated the problem, but the incremental disciplines have not followed. Thousands of children a day still die from easily preventable causes. Although far fewer die from these causes than a few decades ago, it is still an outrage. If we cared to count, we would find that some of the children died within blocks of this pulpit, these pews. At the other end of the human spectrum, millions of elderly live in isolation, pushed onto the margins, out of sight and beyond community. They are wasted as surely as those who die in the desert. And some of them also sit within blocks of us this morning.

Why is it so hard to act? Simply, the things that look easy, but are actually hard, are those things that depend on community, especially community expressed over time in simple acts of mutual caring.

In the last fifty years the productive life expectancy of nearly everyone in the world has been growing at an amazing rate. While everyone has been astounded at the latest computer-driven hospitals in this country, the real revolution has been accomplished through mundane but consistent application of preventive care, mostly applied by teaching people what they can do for themselves. Inexpensive interventions such as immunization extend far more lives than the high-cost machinery in hospitals. Eating smart, avoiding drugs and smoking, wearing seat belts, cleaning the water—these ideas sound boring, but they are extending lives all over the world where they are promoted. This is so well known that we can barely keep our eyes open when we think about it. So why is following this advice so hard?

Choice is not the same as *change*. Revolutionary choice can be announced by individuals. We call these people (when they succeed) prophets, and they deserve all the honor they can get. But truly revolutionary change can only be built by communities, especially communities capable of faithfully nurturing what I call "applied hope."

It is only in hopeful communities that the mundane incremental steps toward the future are supported in their revolutionary implications. People of faith can recognize the linkage between immunizing a baby and the inbreaking of God's eternal hope for the same baby. Life is life! Wherever it is extended and dignified, God breaks in and claims a little more territory back from death. The herald angels hark their loudest: "That's not a needle, it is a virtual cross waved in the face of death!" It is not just a medical event, it is a divine celebration. The same can be said for tutoring, a truly boring and bothersome activity, at first glance, if there ever was one. But where others yawn, God's faithful community laughs because we recognize the very walls of despair crumbling.

Faithful community gives us a lens that puts the world in focus. The incremental and mundane are bathed in God's light so we can see them for what they truly are, as surprising as a refugee king.

My point is simple. I want people to be able to look at our fellowship and see that we are not just about the big choices, but we see God in all the little ones too. I'm comfortable that we are on high ground regarding the big issues. I am far less comfortable about the little things like tutoring and health care in our neighborhood. I am convinced that is exactly where God's revolution is being fought now.

I think Mary and Joseph would point us toward the mundane revolutionary opportunity still surrounding us. The health-care crisis is all over the news. It doesn't matter what kind of reform is suggested because no automatic mechanism can function if we don't look out for each other locally. No system can make community unnecessary. No system can replace human caring.

What if everyone within ten blocks of this corner were well fed every day; every pregnant woman received prenatal care; every elderly person got to his or her doctor; every infant was immunized; everyone of working age received cancer screening and help with smoking or drugs? How mundane. How revolutionary.

Those are all things that, combined, would probably extend the lives of people in our neighborhood by an average of ten years each! I think that's a revolution worth choosing and, more important, one that's worth building. Can we pray together now that this might be? And when we walk out of here this morning, can we allow ourselves to see our neighborhood with newly opened eyes?

GARY GUNDERSON is the director of the Interfaith Health Program of the Rollins School of Public Health at Emory University.

—— 16. ——
My Son Beat Me to the Grave

WILLIAM SLOANE COFFIN JR.

As almost all of you know, on an early January night, while driving in a terrible storm, my son Alexander—who to his friends was a real day-brightener, and to his family "fair as a star when only one is shining in the sky"—my 24-year old Alexander, who enjoyed beating his old man at every game and in every race, beat his father to the grave.

Among the healing flood of letters that followed his death was one carrying this wonderful quote from the end of Hemingway's *A Farewell to Arms*: "The world breaks everyone, then some become strong at the broken places." My own broken heart is mending, and largely thanks to so many of you, my dear parishioners; for if in the last week I have relearned one lesson, it is that love not only begets love, it transmits strength.

Because so many of you have cared so deeply and because obviously I've been able to think of little else, I want this morning to talk of Alex's death, I hope in a way helpful to all.

When a person dies there are many things that can be said, and there is at least one thing that should never be said. The night after Alex died I was sitting in the living room of my sister's house outside of Boston, when the front door opened and in came a nice-looking middle-aged woman, carrying about 18 quiches. When she saw me she shook her head, then headed for the kitchen, saying sadly over her shoulder, "I just don't understand the will of God." Instantly I was up and in hot pursuit, swarming all over her. "I'll say you don't lady!" I said. (I knew the anger would do me good, and the instruction to her was long overdue.) I continued, "Do you think it was the will of God that Alex never fixed that lousy windshield wiper on his car, that he was probably driving too fast in such a storm, that he probably had had a couple of 'frosties' too many? Do you think it is God's will that there are no streetlights along that stretch of road, and no guardrail separating the road and Boston Harbor?"

For some reason, nothing so infuriates me as the incapacity of seemingly intelligent people to get it through their heads that God doesn't go around this world with his finger on triggers, his fist around knives, his hands on steering wheels. God is dead set against all unnatural deaths. And Christ spent an inordinate amount of time delivering people from paralysis, insanity, leprosy and muteness. Which is not to say that there are no nature-caused deaths (I can think of many right here in this parish in the five years I've been here), deaths that are untimely and slow and pain-ridden, which for that reason raise unanswerable questions, and even the specter of a Cosmic Sadist—yes, even an Eternal Vivesector. But violent deaths, such as the one Alex died—to understand those is a piece of cake. As his younger brother put it simply, standing at the head of the casket at the Boston funeral, "You blew it buddy. You blew it." The one thing that should never be said when someone dies is, "It is the will of God." Never do we know enough to say that. My own consolation lies in knowing that it was *not* the will of God that Alex die; that when the waves closed over the sinking car, God's heart was the first of all our hearts to break.

I mentioned the healing flood of letters. Some of the very best, and easily the worst, came from fellow reverends, a few of whom proved they knew their Bibles better than the human condition. I know all the "right" biblical passages, including "Blessed are they who mourn," and my faith is no house of cards; these passages are true, I know. But the point is this: While the words of the Bible are true, grief renders them unreal. The reality of grief is the absence of God—"My God, my God, why hast thou forsaken me?" The reality of grief is the solitude of pain, the feeling that your heart's in pieces, your mind's a blank, that "there is no joy the world can give like that it takes away" (Lord Byron).

That's why immediately after such a tragedy people must come to your rescue, people who only want to hold your hand, not to quote anybody or even say anything, people who simply bring food and flowers—the basics of beauty and life—people who sign letters simply, "Your broken-hearted sister." In other words, in my intense grief I felt some of my fellow reverends—not many and none of you, thank God—were using comforting words of Scripture for self-protection, to pretty up a situation whose bleakness they simply couldn't face. But like God herself, Scripture is not around for anyone's protection, just for everyone's unending support.

And that's what hundreds of you understood so beautifully. You gave me what God gives all of us—minimum protection, maximum support. I swear to you, I wouldn't be standing here were I not upheld.

After the death of his wife, C.S. Lewis wrote, "They say, 'the coward dies many times'; so does the beloved. Didn't the eagle find a fresh liver to tear in Prometheus every time it dined?"

When parents die, as did my mother recently, they take with them a large portion of the past. But when children die, they take away the future as well. That is what makes the valley of the shadow of death seem so incredibly dark and unending. In a prideful way it would be easier to walk the valley alone, nobly, head high, instead of—as we must—marching as the latest recruit in the world's army of the bereaved.

Still there is much by way of consolation. Because there are no rankling unanswered questions, and because Alex and I simply adored each other, the wound for me is deep, but clean. I know how lucky I am. I also know that this day-brightener of a son wouldn't wish to be held close by grief (nor, for that matter, would any but the meanest of our beloved departed), and that, interestingly enough when I mourn Alex least I see him best.

Another consolation, of course, will be the learning—which better be good, given the price. But it's a fact: few of us are naturally profound; we have to be forced down. So while it's true:

> I walked a mile with Pleasure
> She chattered all the way;
> But left me none the wiser
> For all she had to say.
>
> I walked a mile with Sorrow
> And ne'er a word said she;
> But oh, the things I learned from her
> When sorrow walked with me.
> —Robert Browning Hamilton

Or, in Emily Dickinson's verse,

> By a departing light
> We see acuter quite
> Than by a wick that stays.
> There's something in the flight
> That clarifies the sight
> And decks the rays.

And of course I know, even when pain is deep, that God is good. "My God, my God, why hast thou forsaken me?" Yes, but at least, "My God, my God"; and the psalm only begins that way, it doesn't end that way. As the grief that once seemed unbearable begins to turn now to bearable sorrow, the truths in the "right" biblical passages are beginning once again to take hold: "Cast thy burden upon the Lord and he shall strengthen thee"; "Weeping may endure for a night, but joy cometh in the morning"; "Lord, by thy favor thou hast made my mountain to stand strong"; "for thou hast delivered my soul from death, mine eyes from tears, and my feet from falling." "In this world ye shall have tribulation, but be of good cheer, I have overcome the world." "The light shines in the darkness, and the darkness has not overcome it."

And finally I know that when Alex beat me to the grave, the finish line was not Boston Harbor in the middle of the night. If a lamp went out, it was because, for him at least, the Dawn had come.

So I shall—so let us all—seek consolation in that love which never dies, and find peace in the dazzling grace that always is.

WILLIAM SLOANE COFFIN JR. served as chaplain of Yale University during the Vietnam War. He was in early opposition to the war and became famous for his antiwar activities. He was then senior minister at Riverside Church in New York City and then became president of the SANE/FREEZE campaign for global security, the largest peace and justice organization in the United States.

LaVergne, TN USA
16 July 2010
189738LV00001B/29/A